Roll
with it

Roll with it

Encountering grace, grins, gridlock, and God in everyday life

TOM ALLEN

atmosphere press

To my wonderful wife, Cathy, an extremely patient woman from whom I most often encounter grace and grins, and to our stellar offspring, in-law kids, and grandchild: Andy, Amy, Emily, Lauren, Bayron, and Maya. You light up our days.

A Word Before...

I haven't met anyone who's really excited about reading a preface—so number one, I'm not calling it that, and number two, I will be brief. I just wanted to say thanks for giving this book a shot and I hope you'll be encouraged as you read; that you'll find you have something in common with my stumbling, bumbling life, and that you'll chuckle a time or two.

"Either life is holy with meaning, or life doesn't mean a damn thing," says pastor and author Frederick Buechner, and I love that, because it means even our most mundane days offer opportunities to experience a life beyond ourselves. And beyond ourselves is where the really good stuff is.

I also think we're way, way better off when we allow ourselves to enjoy our wander through life as much as possible. I'm a big fan of Darryl Tippens's take on that in his book *Pilgrim Heart*: "God made us playful creatures, and it is proper and honorable to exercise this prized gift."

I'm doing the best I can with both the enjoying and the seeking of the bigger picture. I highly recommend both.

One last thing: The "chapters" that follow are columns published in Virginia newspapers (except for a handful) over the last few years and therefore don't need to be read in any particular order. Do with them what you will!

Tom Allen
Richmond, Virginia
July 2023

"There is no saint without a past,
no sinner without a future."
– St. Augustine

"Humans are not intended for data storage
(though we have that capacity). We are intended for living,
for moving through a story."
– N.D. Wilson

"We are not here to show something to God. We are here
because God—the One who wants to be completely known—
has something to show to us."
– Robert Benson

Table of Contents

.

Who's Steering This Thing?

I have a friend who harbors a deep distrust of restaurant buffets. He wonders how long the food has been sitting out waiting to be eaten, and if it might also have been sitting out yesterday, too. So, he makes a point of bypassing the spreads and always ordering from the menu. One day, he went with some friends to a Chinese restaurant with a daily lunch buffet and, as usual, ordered an entrée instead.

As he watched his buddies start loading up their plates at the buffet, he noticed someone else heading in that direction, too. It was their waiter, who made use of the buffet to dish out what my friend had ordered before bringing the plate happily to the table.

We have so little control.

Sure, a little intervention might have rescued lunch that day and it (probably) wasn't a life-or-death situation, but when it comes to the ultimate things of life, we have remarkably little say. What makes that especially problematic is that we're really, really into being in control. We want to feel like we call our own plays and can take life in a different direction whenever necessary.

We come by this problem naturally, it seems. Tullian Tchividjian, a pastor and author, defines human nature as being "addicted to control."

Two things often develop out of a control addiction, it seems to me, and neither is good. One, it's just exhausting to be constantly orchestrating the circumstances of life. There's always another angle to cover, another possibility to anticipate. There aren't a lot of situations in which you can, with great certainty, nail down the outcome you want ahead of time. But we can run ourselves ragged trying.

Second—and, to me, even more important—something meaningful, life-changing—and absolutely beyond our control—will come along. It will involve a lot more than a menu choice at a restaurant, and we likely won't see it coming. As singer Mat Kearney puts it, "I guess we're all one phone call from our knees."

Life can feel so random. How are we supposed to cope with that?

The only way I know is to just look it in the face. Stuff is going to come at me in life I'd never have chosen. There are phone calls out there for me, too.

I can't do that alone. I have to know that there's someone big enough to absorb it with me and, when necessary, for me. I need to know, too, that person is caring and, ultimately, good.

I know someone like that. "Peace I leave with you," Jesus said. "My peace I give you...do not let your hearts be troubled and do not be afraid."

I *will* be afraid, and my heart *will* be troubled. But I can surrender my control to a God like that, one who also calls himself the source of all life and light and asks us to trust him. In theory, it should be easy to give him that trust because he's good and because control is an illusion, anyway. It's *not* easy, though, because I cling to control and there will be lots that I won't understand. But if I can make headway, I think I'll get closer to living in the faith and freedom Jesus has in mind for us.

"We are meant to be free enough to really love God and one another, but true freedom can happen only if we completely trust in God's ultimate care for us," says author and psychiatrist Gerald May.

It's the "completely" part there that will probably be a struggle to maintain for the rest of my days. The best way forward I've come across lately is the approach of the author of Psalm 37: "Trust in the Lord and do good."

If I can move ahead with a growing trust and a growing desire to do good, I can loosen my grip on my life and I believe all will, in the end, be well. No matter what happens.

Hide and Seek

I grew up in a big family, eventually numbering six children, Mom, Dad, various neighborhood kids, and a succession of animals, including a golden retriever whose housebreaking skills briefly disintegrated after grass-like, green shag carpeting was installed in one of the rooms of the house. The crowd included my littlest sister, who is thirteen years younger than me and who provided a near-constant source of amusement for me before I cleared out after my high school years.

One of her greatest joys when she was three or four was playing hide-and-seek, a game she never tired of even though it always went exactly the same way. She'd stand in the middle of the living room, close her eyes and count as high as she was able, and I'd hide behind the couch, which was approximately four feet away. When she finished counting, she'd open her eyes and yell, "Where are you?"

I'd answer, making no effort to disguise my location, "I'm upstairs!"

She'd bound up the stairs and hunt around, opening a few closet doors before returning to the middle of the living room and announcing, "No, you're not!"

I'd mention the garage or the back porch. Off she'd go. I think I could have said Detroit. But every time, she'd come back to the living room to tell me I was not, actually, where I'd told her I was. In her heart, she knew I was behind the couch; she just didn't realize that she did.

She's not alone. In our hearts, I think we all know a lot more than we realize, too.

So much of what we know is intuitive, something we seem

to just understand. I think, for instance, of the sense that we're born knowing there's a difference between right and wrong, between guilty and innocent, and between kindness and cruelty. No one ever had to tell us not to be cruel to others, cheat in school, or kick a puppy. That doesn't mean that we've necessarily stopped doing those kinds of things—it just means that if we do, we do so knowing deep down that it ain't right.

A conscience, an idea of right and wrong, appears to be a standard item in the human package.

There was an interesting study done a few years ago at Yale University's Infant Cognition Center, widely known as The Baby Lab. Babies less than two years old were shown a puppet show about a gray cat trying to open a box. They saw a bunny wearing green appear and help the cat get the box open. Then they saw an orange-clad bunny come along and slam the box shut, foiling the cat. The babies were then offered the two bunnies simultaneously by a researcher unaware of which was the "good" one. Either by grabbing at or staring at it, more than eighty percent of the tots picked the green bunny.

Does this mean science backs up the idea of us having an inborn sense of right and wrong? Maybe. But lab experiments can't always offer the most meaningful explanations. For that, I think we have to look a bit deeper. If we all just didn't somehow appear here, if we're all born as children of God, then our ultimate source of right and wrong must have been installed by our creator. We arrive knowing, somehow, that we don't get to create our own moral code.

"Right is right even if no one is doing it," is how St. Augustine put it. "Wrong is wrong even if everyone is doing it."

In the Biblical book of 1 Kings, Solomon tells a man who treated another badly, "You know in your heart all the wrong you did." The apostle Paul, writing to the Romans, speaks of even non-believers as having God's law "written on their hearts, their consciences also bearing witness."

Maybe a big part of why we're here is to learn what we've always known.

7

What's In *Your* Bag?

Some years back, my wife and I, along with our then-elementary-school-age kids, took a class at our church called Family Matters. At the first meeting, the couple teaching it nonchalantly asked all the children in the room to name their favorite kind of candy. As the kids answered, notes were quietly taken, but nothing more was said about it for several weeks.

Then one Sunday, we came to class to find a paper bag waiting for each child, and they were instructed to look inside. Each bag contained some of the candy they'd named on week one. Instantly, there was great rejoicing in the land—the children were ecstatic, not only to get the goodies, but because someone had remembered their favorite candy.

Their glee was short-lived. We were then asked to sit in a large circle and all the kids were invited to dump their bags out. Suddenly it was obvious that some kids had received considerably more candy than others. Fairly quickly, the great rejoicing was replaced by a subdued and somewhat grumpy discontent.

The takeaways from class that day: Learn to be grateful for what you have, and "comparison is the enemy of contentment." To this day, there are still a bunch of families around town who exchange knowing smiles at the mention of the slogan from that class session: "What's in *your* bag?"

How about we take a deep breath, without looking around, and just consider the contents of our "bags"? It seems to me that no matter how empty or raggedy some of those bags may sometimes feel, deep within are reasons for gratitude.

I'd like being thankful to be more than an occasional warm and fuzzy sentiment in my world. It deserves to be—and is most true as—a lifestyle. "Gratitude is not a feeling, but an ongoing vision of thank-full-ness that recognizes the gifts constantly being received," say authors Ernest Kurtz and Katherine Ketcham in their book *The Spirituality of Imperfection*.

When I stop and think about it, which I don't often enough do, it's pretty clear that all of life is a gift: The places I go, the legs that carry me there, the people I meet along the way, and, literally, every breath I take. The leaves we watch change their colors, a spectacular sky, the twinkle in a loved one's eye; it's all just given to us.

You can't buy that stuff.

Gratitude also makes the most sense, to me, when it's directed toward someone—just the fact that I feel grateful seems to imply a giver. The biblical book of James says, "Every good and perfect gift is from above, and comes down from the Father of lights." Every day is also an opportunity for me to acknowledge the Source of all that shines and reflects that brightness in my life.

Elie Wiesel, who survived the horrors of the Holocaust to become an author and a Nobel Peace Prize winner, said this in his speech accepting the Nobel: "We know that every moment is a moment of grace, every hour an offering."

Wiesel's sentiment is brought home in an old story about a conversation between a spiritual teacher and a student, told by writer Brennan Manning.

"What must I do to become fully enlightened?" the student asks one day.

The teacher answers with one word: "Awareness."

Puzzled, the student asks for a bit more detail.

"Awareness, awareness, awareness, awareness," responds the teacher.

I suspect that was not the elaboration the student was hoping for. But the teacher's point, I think, is that we almost can't help but experience gratitude when we actually look around and see who and what surrounds us, even when life seems fraught with obstacles and pain.

There's always something in the bag.

The Best-Laid Plans...
Get Destroyed

In the Bible, Proverbs says, "You can make many plans, but the Lord's purpose will prevail." The Bible don't lie.

My folks are in their eighties now and, predictably, experiencing some health challenges. Last year was especially tough on Mom, who fell several times, earning a trip to the emergency room each time.

I hadn't seen them in several months because, well, COVID, so I decided I'd go up to their place in Pennsylvania to check on them. I also thought it would be fun to make the trip a surprise.

Turns out, not such an excellent idea.

I recruited plenty of undercover help for my devious plan, including my sister, Vicki, who lives near Mom and Dad, and my parents' old friend, Lorraine. On many Friday nights, Lorraine and my folks go out for pizza, so on Monday of the week I was planning to show up on Friday, I called her and asked her to nail down the pizza date.

"I can't call this early," Lorraine told me. "She'll be suspicious. I'll call her Thursday."

Fair enough. She also gave me the name of the pizza place where they hang out, so I made a call. The manager got on the phone and when I told him I'd like to pose as my parents' and Lorraine's waiter, to my very great surprise, he agreed to play along. Vicki was to pick me up at the train station and get me to the restaurant. I was very pumped about this, and because the wait staff was required to wear masks and Mom and Dad wouldn't be expecting anything out of the ordinary, I thought maybe I'd get as far as getting their drink order before my cover was blown.

I'll never know. As the train rolled into Washington, D.C., Friday morning, Lorraine called me to say that Mom didn't want to go out. Not sure if it was her concern about COVID or if she was worried about her balance; either way, Friday night pizza got nixed. Crestfallen, I made a quick call to the restaurant and canceled my reservation.

It was time for Plan B.

Mom's last fall had left her with some dizziness and balance issues, so she was scheduled to begin physical therapy the following week. To prepare, the PT practice was sending someone to the house to evaluate her Saturday morning. I'd borrowed some scrubs and brought them along to impersonate a physical therapist, so Vicki got a friend to call my parents and tell them that due to a scheduling mix-up, the PT evaluation was now set for 5 p.m. Friday. "Ryan" would be coming. I hoped to at least get into the house, again masked, before they figured out what was going on.

"They're not happy about the change, though," Vicki warned as the train chugged into Baltimore.

"I hope Mom doesn't call and talk to them about it," I laughed.

Not actually all that funny, as it turns out. Mom did decide it would be best to follow up with the PT practice, who, of course, had no idea what she was talking about. Their confusion convinced her she was being at least scammed, perhaps worse.

Vicki gave me the PT folks' number and I quickly called. For the second time in my quest, I got unexpected cooperation. The woman I spoke with laughed heartily at the plan and assured me she'd try to smooth things out with Mom.

Sadly, there was nothing she could do. She called me back not long after to let me know that when she spoke with Mom, Mom told her that if anyone showed up that afternoon, she'd call the police.

So the jig was up. There would be no surprise. For Mom's sanity, she and Dad had to be let in on the plans and how they'd inadvertently but completely foiled them. Vicki broke the news. We had a great visit anyway.

The moral of the story? I have no idea. But next visit, I'm thinking about hiring a skywriter to give them proper notice that I'm coming.

They Made
Their Innings Count

We went to a minor league baseball game one Saturday night mostly because we wanted to see the fireworks afterward. I'm not sure I could have named a player on the Flying Squirrels before the game, and since baseball isn't really our favorite spectator sport, we grabbed dinner first and rolled in during the bottom of the fifth inning. Perfect.

None of us knew it was also Military Appreciation Night. I noticed the home team wearing uniform shirts with some camouflage on the sleeves, but was confused by the fact that the players' names weren't on the back. Someone else's name was there. Maybe they were throwback jerseys, I thought.

What they really were became clear when the game wrapped up and the players and other team officials took their places in a long line up the chalk leading to and beyond first base. An even longer line of other people gathered along the third-base line.

What happened next brought many to tears, both on the field and in the stands. One by one, the team walked to home plate, met with small groups of folks from the third-base line, and presented them with the jerseys they'd worn during the game. The names on those jerseys were the names of men and women who'd lost their lives or been wounded serving in our country's armed forces. Family members and friends accepted the shirts in honor of lost loved ones; many of the wounded were there to receive theirs in person.

The importance of sacrifice and the beauty and nobility of putting ourselves out there for others doesn't seem to get much attention in our all-about-me culture. For more than 8,000 of us that night, sacrifice came—figuratively and almost literally—out of left field.

Much of the important stuff in life, I think, isn't stuff we need to be told about so much as reminded of. That ceremony was a great (and stark) reminder of what sacrifice means, because if we've been around a few years, most of us have come to understand that real fulfillment happens when we put the needs of others ahead of our own.

"The more we give of ourselves, the more we know who we are," is how Jesuit author James Martin puts it, "and the fuller lives we lead."

That's beautiful. And it's true, but so is this: Many of us are aware that there's a sometimes-yawning chasm in our lives between knowing the truth and consistently acting on it.

"We have an innate tendency toward selfishness," writes *New York Times* columnist and author David Brooks. "We know what's deep and important in life, but we still pursue the things that are shallow and vain."

By "shallow and vain," I think Brooks means "things we think will make us happy even if the consequences for others aren't necessarily awesome."

Our natural self-centeredness makes the sacrifices that have been made for me all the more meaningful. My parents made numerous sacrifices to make my life better. My wife does it every day. Family members, friends, and co-workers have gone out of their way for me. It's gratifying, humbling, and sometimes a bit puzzling.

But I think it's what we're born to do. It just takes some of us very long time to figure it out. There have been occasions when doing something for someone else that cost me time, trouble, or heartache has given me a joy like no other I've known. I've wondered why that feeling hasn't spurred me to make doing those kinds of things a more frequent occurrence.

I'm guessing it has something to do with the "innate selfishness" Brooks speaks of.

Those of us who claim to follow Jesus have an eternal example and reminder of the ultimate in unselfishness, though. His life- and freedom-giving sacrifice at the cross is the clearest demonstration of the meaning and power of sacrifice we'll ever get.

And it's way cooler than even postgame fireworks.

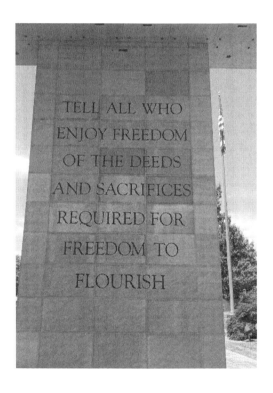

Yo Mama and Me

My oldest daughter was teaching high school Spanish in another state and one day, two of her students, freshman boys, got into an altercation in the hallway. There was shoving and glaring, and rubberneckers were beginning to gather, but no real fisticuffs broke out.

In her school, just about all such incidents also involved a significant amount of verbal abuse, most often the kind focusing on the other combatant's mother. This run-in was no exception, and the boys were letting loose with some fairly creative language, unprintable here, expounding upon their less-than-glowing opinions of the other's "mama."

Nothing terribly unusual—until your daughter mentions that the boys in this conflict are twins.

After the fireworks were over, she—and I imagine others nearby—were wondering at what point it might have dawned on the boys that there weren't two women being bad-mouthed—just one. I'm guessing that beneath the bluster they knew full well they were doing a spectacularly dumb thing, but, because of peer pressure, the heat of the moment, or whatever, they just picked up speed and didn't stop.

Unfortunately, it won't be the last time they, or any of us, do something we know full well is a dumb thing to do, because of peer pressure, the heat of the moment, or whatever.

Very few of us may have actually publicly insulted Mom, but think about it: How many times have we pushed aside our own better judgment for a moment and given into the temptation to do something we know isn't smart? Or kind? Or loving? Or at all constructive? We say things we know are hurtful, often to the last people on earth we'd want to hurt. We do

17

things, or don't do them, because we know people are watching. Or, perhaps more often, because we know they aren't. We don't offer a helping hand because we're not in the mood. And afterward, we wonder why.

The apostle Paul, one of the giants of the early Christian church and author of about half the books in today's New Testament, understood very well this feeling of frustration with one's own actions. "I don't really understand myself," he wrote to first-century Christians in Rome. "I want to do what's right, but I don't do it. Instead, I do what I hate...I want to do what is good, but I don't. I don't want to do what is wrong, but I do it anyway."

So do we. Lately, police have set up an automatic speed-reading sign along a road I take to work most mornings. The speed limit there is 30 (it's a four-lane road and almost no one goes 30). The sign tells you how fast you're going as you approach it, and if you're going over 30, your speed number and the entire border of lights around it begin to blink. Pretty brightly, too. I sometimes find myself (and I'm not alone in this, I've observed) speeding up as I get near the sign, just so I can set it to blinking.

Now, what sense does that make? What is in us that makes us determined to see if that "Keep Off the Grass" sign really applies to us? Why did the ex-husband of a friend sometimes lie to her about where he was or what he was doing, even when he wasn't somewhere he shouldn't have been?

We do dumb things, and we do them pretty regularly, too.

In the same letter to the Romans, Paul calls it what it is: sin. And he adds that none of us is immune. "For everyone has sinned," he writes. "We all fall short." He's got the backing of Jesus on this one, too. Jesus came and got, shall we say, a less than warm reception, at least in part because he called sin what it is, saying, "God's light came into the world, but people loved the darkness more than the light, for their actions were evil."

Much like those ninth-grade boys, who understood at some level that what they were doing was wrong, I think we understand at some level that we need forgiveness. We sense it. We feel it. We know it. And, fortunately, I think we know where to find it.

In Which We Acquire a Rap Sheet

It was a spectacular summer day in Richmond; a Saturday in 1983 with the sky an incredible blue, the clouds huge, and the breeze blowing just enough to tone down the heat. All in all, it was a near-perfect day to be arrested.

One should not squander these opportunities.

Tim, Judy, and I were pedaling our bikes around near the north end of the Huguenot Bridge and, while we were thoroughly enjoying the ride, we were a bit frustrated by our inability to get to the river, our ultimate goal. Everything was private property. So, in the kind of smooth move often made by inexperienced lawbreakers, we decided to park our bikes in the woods along a road and cut through to the river on foot, ignoring the semi-blatant "No Trespassing" sign on a nearby tree. Our mission was accomplished, and we'd been sitting in the sun along the riverbank for a while when our solitude was interrupted by a county police officer, who emerged from the woods to inform us that we were under arrest.

"Are you serious?" we asked, more than a bit naively.

He indicated that he was, indeed, quite serious, and then offered us the choice of doing the arrest paperwork at his car or being brought down to the station to do so. We mulled that for approximately a nanosecond before going for the "do it at the car" option.

According to our newly signed forms, we were now officially charged with trespassing and faced a court date a few weeks later. *A perfectly reasonable explanation will get us out of this*, I thought, and so I found the number of the property's owner and rang him up. I gave what I thought was a stirring defense of our innocent mistake, only to be told by the very nice gentleman, quite rightly, that if he dropped the charges, "the police will never enforce my sign again."

That left us no choice but to throw ourselves upon the mercy of the court. There, a judge calmly listened to our story and promptly convicted us because we were, well, guilty. He did, however, take pity on us and decided not to assess a major fine, sentencing us only to $40 in court costs each.

We were quickly treated to the benefits of our new legal status. They took us to an office to pay our $40, and we got out our checkbooks (it was 1983, remember), only to be told that the county didn't accept checks "from convicted criminals." As it turns out, I was the only one of us that had enough cash with me to pay. My friends remained in custody until I went to an ATM and brought back cash for them. It's fun to think, once in a while, where Tim and Judy might be today if I'd just gone on home.

I thought about our bike outing, the law, and the importance of obeying it recently when I came across this in the Old Testament book of Leviticus: "If you obey my decrees and my regulations, you will find life through them." This was God, speaking to his people as they wandered in the Middle Eastern desert for several decades.

To me, the point here is not the specific regulations given in Leviticus; it was a very different time and culture and we've rightfully moved on from many of them. The issue is that God hasn't given us his metaphorical "No Trespassing" signs to hem us in, keep us in straight lines, and generally be a major buzzkill. His laws and commands are actually about giving us life. Who knows better how to live fully and completely than the one who created life in the first place?

The word "obedience" has very much fallen from favor these days, but maybe because it's become misused and misunderstood. Jesus says the two greatest commandments are to love God and to love one another. Don't most of our problems today stem from our difficulties obeying them?

What if obedience, instead of confining us, sets us free? What if we could put aside our natural distaste for obeying someone other than ourselves? Would we discover that obedience is the path to real adventure and true life?

At the very least, it might make for a shorter rap sheet.

If This Is True...

As the waiter finished refilling our drinks and headed back toward the kitchen, my friend looked across the table and asked a question. "What would my life look like," he said, "if I believed in God—I mean *really* believed in God?"

This is a guy whose life already looks—to just about everybody—like that of a pretty firm believer. He's been part of a church for a long time and over the years I've seen him and his wife reach out to and care for people in amazing ways. But he, like pretty much everyone else I've ever met, still has struggles and questions about faith, what it means, and how it plays out in "real" life.

If he or I truly accept that there's a God and that he is absolutely real—as real as my wife sitting on the couch in the next room as I type—how would that change us? Should I go on living life the same way I always have? What if, beyond the niceties we may have heard (and maybe parroted, perhaps ignored) for years, there's really, truly, and actually a God who created everything we see, feel, and know?

Including me.

It's kind of a big deal. "Once you accept the existence of God, however you define him, however you explain your relationship to him," said novelist Morris West, "then you are caught forever with his presence in the center of all things."

That's pretty all-encompassing.

Well-known priest and writer Henri Nouwen didn't downplay the matter of God, either. "To say with all we have, think, feel and are, 'God exists,' is the most world-shattering statement a human being can make," he wrote.

West and Nouwen, a couple of profound and widely-respected thinkers, believe the stakes are pretty high. Do I?

I race through a lot of my days preoccupied with the illusion that I'm running my own show, and many times lose God in my deadlines, appointments, technology or, simply, the pace of activities. On those days, maybe he'll come to mind if something significantly worrisome comes up. How meaningful is that, really?

There's no shortage of perspectives on God and how he might operate. Christianity teaches that God's son came to Earth and died on our behalf. Judaism believes that the Messiah has not yet arrived. Buddhism and Hinduism don't really focus on God as a being, but believe we can attain enlightenment through a series of reincarnations. Islam believes Jesus was a prophet, not actually God, and that Mohammed is at least his equal.

There are also different schools of thought on the role God plays these days. Some think that while he created us, he's likely busy doing other divine things and not really involved in our daily lives. Others think he's paying attention, but mostly as a fairly passive spectator. Still others believe in a God who is intimately involved with us in every moment and knows us even better than we know ourselves.

How should any of this affect the way we approach our days? I think my friend was feeling a little of that and it made him wonder, as someone who claims and wants to believe in God, if his life looks any different than anyone else's. If you're a believer, does that faith factor into decisions about how you spend time, who you hang out with, what you choose as entertainment, or how you spend money?

I am a Christian, but sometimes I wonder, like my friend, how deep into my core I allow my faith to go and how accurately my life reflects it.

If God is real, and so is my faith, I believe it should change me. I should be a better person because of it, not because I'm required to be or because I'm afraid bad things will happen to me if I'm not—but because I want to.

I'd like my primary response when I think about a real and living God not to be fear or obligation, but gratitude.

Keeping "the Boy" Alive

When my mother-in-law pulled out of our driveway after spending a week with us following the birth of our first child, we were, let's say, a little freaked out. "What are we supposed to do with the boy?" we asked frantically, looking around the now-empty house for someone to answer. We'd never even had a pet, unless you count Seymour, the recently-given-away parakeet.

We felt this way even though my wife was a baby nurse with years of hospital experience. Without her, I'm pretty sure I would have immediately left the country. I shudder to think what bringing home a baby must be like for parents who are regular, non-medical types, of which I am a card-carrying member.

We managed to feed and mostly clothe the boy for a while, but weren't fully convinced he'd ever overcome his parenting.

At first, he gave regular indications that we might be right. On a vacation trip we took when he was a preschooler, we took him fishing on the dock of a lake one evening, with extremely limited success (which is to say, none at all). We returned to the dock the next afternoon to do the much easier activity of tossing bread to ducks. A bunch of the neighborhood fish also showed up for the buffet, prompting the boy to look at us and say, very matter-of-factly, "A lot of these fish are probably here because they remember me from last night."

Not long after, the boy developed a fascination with dinosaurs that occupied most of his waking hours. About this time, the Science Museum announced what I thought was a most appropriate exhibit for a father-son outing—large, motorized dinosaurs. It was not the kind of parenting decision one reads about in advice columns. If there was ever a more terrified kindergartner, I've never come across him. The adventure set his sleeping habits back a good year or two.

In early elementary school, the boy volunteered to take custody of the class pet for the Christmas holidays. The "pet" was a bit over-fed crayfish named Fidgety, which came home in a Tupperware transport—a much more confining environment than the classroom tank it normally inhabited. We had no tank, so the Tupperware became a winter vacation home. It was okay lengthwise, but when Fidgety tried to turn himself around, he'd usually come face-to-face with unyielding plastic (did I mention he was a little over-fed?). We didn't understand the gravity of this issue. So, many of the particles involved in the boy's faithful Fidgety feedings apparently floated out of the poor crustacean's reach, resulting in his soon-after-coming-home demise. That, in turn, resulted in a frozen winter day funeral, observed through a window in our home by three wailing youngsters (the boy and his two younger sisters). A bundled-up Mom did the undertaking honors, as I had fled to the office.

The boy recovered, then proceeded to age to the point where the state of Virginia deemed him mature enough to receive his very own driving learner's permit. This was, perhaps, premature. We went for a spin one day not far from home and I casually mentioned to him that he might need to "eventually" get in the left lane, as we'd be turning at the traffic light, which was still approximately a half-mile ahead. He took my instructions to heart—immediately. The lane was changed, minus a turn signal or any significant glance in the mirror. While no actual bumper cars were played, the boy did get his first digital greeting from a fellow "driver" that day.

The boy is married now.

He's 6'6", does way better growing facial hair than I ever have, and owns a home. He's lived in Louisiana for the last seven years. We laugh like old friends when we talk and, sometimes, have serious discussions about things that matter. To the best of my knowledge, he no longer flees fake dinosaurs and has begun to use turn signals. He's become the man we could never have imagined, someone who had never crossed our minds the day my mother-in-law headed home, and one of whom we're ridiculously proud. I cherish our relationship as adults.

Still, he'll always be "the boy" to me.

Birds of "Pray"

Not long ago, a friend was attempting to work through some significant struggles, both personal and professional.

During one largely sleepless night, his mind settled on something he remembered Jesus saying about anxiety: "Look at the birds. They don't plant or harvest or store food in barns, for your heavenly Father feeds them. And aren't you far more valuable to him than they are?"

Reassured, his fretting subsided and he drifted off to sleep.

On his drive to work the next morning, he spotted a bird on a tree branch along the road, admired it, and remembered Jesus' words from the previous night. As he watched, the bird swooped gracefully down from its perch—and promptly was hit by the car in front of him.

Okay, the irony of all that, when he told several of us the next day, had us in near-uproarious laughter.

But after a few minutes, it wasn't so funny—we were left, as we are so often in matters of faith, with something of a paradox. Yes, we have a loving Father whose care for us is so great that he knows the number of hairs on our heads. But that wonderful fact is not accompanied by any guarantees that some very bad things won't happen in this life.

In fact, it's quite the opposite—we're assured by no less than Jesus himself that "in this world you will have trouble."

As usual, he's quite right.

There was trouble one summer weekend as I sat on a beach in South Carolina with my sister, watching the moon and stars slowly come out and talking about that morning's funeral for her ex-husband. I know she and their two children have had moments of feeling like they had swooped, unknowingly, into oncoming traffic.

There was trouble, too, a couple of weeks before that, as we stood with another side of the family as they buried their twenty-five-year-old daughter, who had struggled for many years with disease and disability. Oncoming traffic, again.

An awful lot goes wrong in this world. What are we supposed to make of that?

The best short answer I can give is, "I don't really know." And while on the face of it, that answer may seem to leave us alone and adrift, I find a kind of freedom in it. I'm not the all-knowing answer man; I've tried to let go of the pressure of having to be able to explain away everything.

I can't do that, and I never will. I've come to realize that the path to peace, for me, is to yield that power to someone far greater than me, someone who can actually handle it. That feels liberating.

No one escapes the suffering and loss that are part of the human experience but, in the midst of the pain, there also seems to be opportunity.

"Suffering invites us to place our hurts in larger hands," Henri Nouwen writes. The challenge comes in learning to trust those hands.

I think a great deal of my own suffering can be traced to my lifelong and hopelessly determined desire to control life. Control gives us a sense of order and security, but it's an illusory one. The words "control" and "surrender" have become very meaningful to me. My theory is that just about all of us are control freaks—the only difference is how committed we are to being one.

And suffering and loss are, perhaps, the ultimate pieces of evidence pointing to what little control we really have.

Nouwen again: "God invites us to experience our not being in control as an invitation to faith."

That's an uncomfortable invitation, because such a faith

must include grappling with our total inability to classify and fully understand God. We are not, however, at a complete loss. From where I stand, God has revealed more than enough information to provide what I most need: hope.

I need hope when life is ugly, dark, lonely, and scary. I need hope that in the end, as Julian of Norwich said, "All will be well." I need hope for funerals, and even for low-flying birds.

Fortunately, Jesus gives me some. He wasn't done talking when he told us we'd have trouble in this world. In his very next breath, he said, "But take heart! I have overcome the world."

Roadside Assistance

Just for the record, I'd like to say that I'm not getting paid for what I'm putting in the next three paragraphs.

Now then: In my humble opinion, AAA is in the top ten greatest organizations on the planet. With its round-the-clock number and ability to summon automotive wizards to the scene of trouble in about an hour, AAA has saved the day for me and my family members more times than I can tell.

Over the years, Cathy, the kids, and I haven't typically been behind the wheel of cars most would describe as "late model." Thus, I've twice had the opportunity to experience the significantly desolate feeling of standing along the shoulder of Interstate 95, marooned with a vehicle that has decided, for a shredded tire or whatever reason, that it can go no farther. It's a little like being on a desert island, only with the potential rescue ships blowing by at something like 70 mph and not glancing in your direction. The difference is you get to call the magic phone number and, before long, a wizard (or wizardess) comes by in a truck.

We've also had dead batteries, keys locked inside cars, alternators that went belly-up, and a host of other ailments that have required punching up AAA's 800 number. So, when they hit me up for renewal, I can't write the check fast enough.

Because sometimes we all need a little roadside assistance.

As COVID-19 came rumbling through, more and more of us found ourselves feeling somehow marooned. And, happily, more and more folks seem to be willing to play the part of the roadside wizard. Some of them make the news; many more do not. Here's some of what I've seen going on, just in my small, semi-quarantine world:

One friend got tired of reading about how disastrous the situation was getting at a local rehabilitation and care center and set out to do something for its beleaguered staff. She and her two children put the word out to friends and then on social media, and were a bit mind-boggled by the response. They ended up being able to prepare gift bags, including a Kroger gift card and numerous other goodies, for all 100-plus center employees.

In the face of this pandemic's widespread misfortune and grief, it's hard to know how to help, or to feel like we're making any difference. Cumulatively, I think, we sure are. Other folks we know are doing whatever small things they can: using their stimulus checks to support local businesses in any way they can, checking with neighbors when heading for the grocery store to see what they might need, looking in on elderly friends and family members, and generally trying to strengthen the bonds we feel (some who hadn't heard of it months ago have suddenly become Zoom gurus).

Many are motivated by their faith; by the call of Jesus to care for our neighbor. I haven't found anywhere in the Bible where He used the word "wizard," but he was very big on looking out for others. And his brother, James, wrote this in the New Testament: "What good is it, dear brothers and sisters, if you say you have faith but don't show it by your actions? ... Suppose you see a brother or sister who has no food or clothing and you say, 'Goodbye and have a good day; stay warm and eat well'—but then you don't give that person any food or clothing? What good does that do?"

It's been good to see folks doing good.

Some of us seem bent on what we can *get* in life; others seem to lean more toward what we can *give*. Truth is, there are plenty of both of those outlooks in all of us. COVID seems to be bringing out the "give" in many. Many are actively looking out for each other in ways we might not under ordinary circumstances. That's been a beautiful thing, and one I hope can be a lasting, positive legacy of this virus.

Because, pandemic or not, sometimes we all need a little roadside assistance.

The Way We Were

I was grabbing a quick sandwich and eased into a booth next to two women who were already well into their lunch. One looked to be in her eighties and the other in her fifties or sixties, and as the conversation went on, I guessed they were mother and daughter.

I wasn't trying to eavesdrop, but I couldn't help hearing when the older woman broke a short silence.

"Where is Frederick?" she asked.

Gently, the younger woman responded, "Frederick died six years ago."

"That's a long time," said the older woman. She paused, then added, "Now, Frederick is the gentleman I was married to, right?"

"Yes, he was," was the response. "He died when you were still living at the house."

Again, the older woman paused. "Where do I live now?" she asked.

I wanted to cry into my potato salad.

The conversation that followed was an almost unbearable litany of information provided by the younger woman, attempting to jog the older woman's memory: the name of the retirement community where she now lives, which family members and friends are still alive, who sometimes comes to visit her, and where the two of them were headed after lunch.

I don't know enough about medicine to say for sure that this woman was suffering from Alzheimer's Disease, but the odds are she was. Alzheimer's is responsible for about sixty to eighty percent of dementia cases, according to the Alzheimer's

Association. It doesn't really matter to me, as a non-medical person, what you call it. Alzheimer's and dementia in all its forms are cruel and unfeeling afflictions—they rob men and women of precious and irreplaceable qualities, like their relationships, their memories, their ability to understand what's going on around them, and even their personalities.

Alzheimer's has now taken Frederick from this woman, along with her images of the home they shared and who knows what else. Even if she doesn't understand that well enough to be pained by it, it certainly must pain the kind and patient woman I took to be her daughter. And I made a point of glancing at the older woman as I left the restaurant—just from seeing her, you'd have no idea of the struggle her life has become.

There's so much I didn't know about Alzheimer's and dementia. The Centers for Disease Control says, for instance, that Alzheimer's is the sixth leading cause of death in the United States. To me, it stands out on their list, which includes ailments like heart disease, cancer, and strokes. We have some ways to combat those health issues, and people regularly go through treatment and recover from them. No one recovers from Alzheimer's. There is no cure at the moment, only some medications that seem to slow the disease's progress. Research is progressing, but no one knows when—or if—we'll be able to do anything about Alzheimer's.

As more and more of us live longer, more of us will also face dementia, in whatever form it comes. It robs the rest of us, too; we need the wisdom, compassion, and experience of our elders. And they deserve to live their final years in dignity.

Some of us like to think that a lack of a family history of Alzheimer's is a kind of shield, preventing us from getting it. The truth is that Alzheimer's doesn't discriminate. If you currently are in possession of a brain, you're at risk.

As I move further into my sixties, my friends and I forget things and sometimes joke that it must be the onset of Alzheimer's. But there's actually nothing funny about it. The woman from the next booth in the deli that day is probably looking at a gradual process that began with forgetfulness, progressed to dementia, and will likely move on to a walker, a wheelchair, specialized care in a nursing home, an increasing inability to understand her surroundings, and death. Her family will have to accompany her through that terrible process.

We really must find a cure.

Joining the Secret Service

A friend was visiting his gravely ill father in the hospital one afternoon and, when other family members and friends had left, found himself alone in the room with him. The father wasn't really able to communicate, but my friend decided, as he later explained, "to just be there with him and for him," and remained quietly at his bedside.

As he sat with his father, he says he felt a presence and peace in the room he'd never quite felt before. He felt something clearly beyond himself, and while there was no dramatic change in his father's condition that day, I think the experience may have changed my friend a little.

There is a certain kind of joy that comes with complete selflessness—when you give of yourself to someone and maybe no one else even knows about it, including the recipient, and you do it expecting nothing in return. "Secret service" may, in fact, be the purest form of joy there is.

Jesus was a big fan of this kind of attention-deflecting caring for our neighbor. "When you give to someone in need," he said, "don't do as the hypocrites do—blowing trumpets in the streets to call attention to their acts of charity! ... When you give to someone in need, don't let your left hand know what your right hand is doing. Give your gifts in private and your Father, who sees everything, will reward you."

I've seen some excellent examples of folks getting creative with doing good with one hand while keeping the other in the dark about it, and it's been almost as much fun to see or hear about as it must have been to do.

A co-worker at a job I once had was struggling with coming back to work after the birth of her second child. When work stress had piled up before this maternity leave, she'd developed a habit of walking to a nearby ice cream shop and getting a milkshake. It never failed to make her day a much better one. One afternoon, not long after she returned to work, she had her office door shut, a telltale sign that things were probably not going very well. Another co-worker spotted the closed door, disappeared for a bit, and returned with a milkshake. He placed it on the floor outside her door, gently knocked, then slipped away.

Her door stayed open the rest of the day.

Another guy I know will occasionally get a cashier's check at the bank, the kind that doesn't have his name on it, and send it to someone he knows is struggling financially. I'm betting those folks had a leave-their-door-open kind of feeling at the mailbox on those days. Another man was told about a program started by some restaurants in other states and has begun encouraging local restaurants to adopt it. It's a pay-it-forward opportunity in which customers, when paying for their meals, can also purchase coupons to be applied to the bills of other customers who may need the help. I've also seen folks anonymously buy police officers' meals in restaurants. I think the look on one officer's face on a Thursday morning made everyone in the restaurant's day.

This one isn't as anonymous, but still made for a good time: A couple I know was standing in a very long line at an out-of-town art museum a few years back when a stranger walked by and handed them two free tickets to the featured exhibit. It saved the pair both time and money—and left them big, unexpected grins on their faces.

Rick Warren, author of the record-breaking bestseller *The Purpose Driven Life*, has said that his book is countercultural and so he thought he'd start it with the most countercultural statement he could come up with. The book's opening? "It's not about you."

That's why I think the biggest grin outside the art museum

that day may actually have belonged to the stranger who gave away his tickets. As Nobel Prize winner Desmond Tutu puts it, "Selflessness opens a door to real peace."

Kiddos, Start Your Mowers!

In addition to having someone to do yard work, one of the big reasons my wife and I had kids was to provide some comic relief around the house. A couple decades into the parenthood thing, the kids and their friends *have* been good for a lot of laughs—which is great because, frankly, we've gotten very little yard work out of them.

The fun started pretty quickly. When our firstborn, Andy, was six, I coached his soccer team, and we spent the fall getting clobbered every Saturday by teams of other six-year-olds who were clearly better coached. During one game, I gathered all eight team members around me on the grass for a highly inspirational halftime chat. They listened intently, and I silently congratulated myself for getting through to them so well. As I wrapped up, one little girl raised her hand.

"Yes, Katie?" I said, fully prepared for a thoughtful question about our second-half strategy.

"The other morning, I had to run for the school bus, but I made it," she announced gravely. While I did permanent damage to my face as I tried not to burst out laughing, Andy and the rest of the team nodded in understanding, like this was one of the most logical things one could say during a soccer game.

Logic also surfaced one night when all three of the kids—who were now in elementary school—and I found ourselves at a restaurant for dinner while my wife was at work. Andy said something about how our vacuum cleaner really "sucks stuff up," and was immediately informed by Emily, our youngest, that "sucks" is a bad word. Smarty-pants Amy, the middle child, seized the teachable moment.

"It just depends on how you use it," she said. "It's kinda like this: If you're talking about a donkey, it's okay to say..." and went on to announce, quite smugly, a three-letter word beginning with an A that is indeed a synonym for donkey—and was indeed heard by a good portion of our fellow IHOP diners.

I couldn't argue with her.

Today, Amy is a Spanish teacher in an inner-city high school in another state, and is still seizing those teachable moments. She has a freshman in one of her classes who seems to enjoy sharing his flatulence issues with the class. So, one night Amy added a spray bottle of Lysol air freshener to her school supplies and now, whenever there's an "issue," she grabs the bottle and gives the young man's immediate environment a thorough spraying. Word of this strategy has spread, and now other teachers have begun sending students to her classroom to borrow the Lysol when this young man is in one of their classes.

Teaching the kids to drive was also highly entertaining, in much the same way that some people really enjoyed the

Freddy Krueger movies. One day I was riding shotgun with Andy, who'd recently acquired a learner's permit. We were on a four-lane road and I mentioned to him that he should think about getting in the left lane because we would be turning left at the next traffic light, still a good mile ahead.

Immediately and obediently, he changed lanes. No signal. No checking the mirror. No nothing. Now, normally I'm in favor of immediate obedience when I ask the kids to do something, although I can think of a few exceptions. Like then, for instance. I'm not sure exactly what came out of my mouth, but I don't think anyone would have mistaken it for gentle encouragement.

Fortunately, the closest car in the left lane had enough time to make room for us, but Andy did receive his first "digital" salute from another driver that day.

And that's not all the illegal activity the kids have gotten into in an attempt to amuse their parents. One day in high school, Emily slipped a nauseous friend a...Tums. For this, the young miscreant soon found herself having to explain her actions in the principal's office. Apparently, Tums is a widely known "gateway drug" and almost inevitably leads to the hard stuff: Pepto-Bismol and even Mylanta.

We managed to spring her.

Children really are, as the Bible says, a gift from the Lord, and the kids have truly proved to be an excellent source of entertainment over the years.

Bet they would have been outstanding with rakes, too.

Siblings Everywhere

Barbara used to run the homeless shelter, and one afternoon I got to hang around and see her do it. As we sat in her office, the children of some of the residents came by to show her their schoolwork, adults came and went with questions, and one woman called to report on the trip she was taking with the bus fare Barbara had given her earlier in the day.

At one point, we were interrupted by another call and I listened to Barbara question the person on the other end of the phone. "How many children?" "How old are they?" "Do

 you have transportation?" And, finally, "I'll see you when you get here."

In the semi-controlled chaos that was that afternoon, what I remember most is Barbara, talking about the motley crew of residents that come and go, smiled and said, "We're all God's children."

I thought about her and her approach to caring for downtrodden folks after a recent stop at a gas station in a part of town I'm not often in. The pump wasn't cooperating with my credit card, and I was trying to figure out what to do when a man rode up to me on a significantly beat-up bicycle.

He was somewhere in his fifties or sixties, I guessed, and had the same grizzled, lots-of-hard-miles-on-him look that the bike did. He was also clearly unhappy. Sullenly, he looked at both me and my wallet intently, then opened the conversation with, "We buried my mother this morning…"

In certain parts of town (actually, there are more and more of those parts), you get approached by down-on-their-luck folks. Some come with elaborate stories, so I was immediately a little dubious, but expressed my sympathy. He told me he was from North Carolina and could use a little cash, so I fished a couple of ones out of my wallet and offered them to him. "If you give me that five, too, I can get a whole meal," he said, gesturing toward a nearby fast-food restaurant.

To be honest, his approach and tone were a little unsettling and a tad intimidating. I handed him the ones, declining his request for extra money. Just as unhappily as he'd arrived, and without a word, he pedaled off.

The pump still wouldn't take my credit card, so I pulled around to another one. I'd barely swiped the card when a teenager walked over and launched into a spiel about the worthy cause he was seeking money for. A little frustrated at being hit up for cash again, I brushed him off, probably somewhat less than graciously, and finished pumping my gas.

Moments later, I pulled out of the station and my radio offered me these lyrics from a "what I'd do different" kind of song playing at that moment:

"I'd love like I'm not scared, give when it's not fair;
Live life for another, take time for a brother…"

My faith leaves room for God to speak in lots of ways, and sometimes I wonder if there's really any such thing as a coincidence. Truth is, I *was* a little scared. And sure, it wasn't necessarily fair to be approached that way. But the man is, indeed, a brother. And, apparently, one in need.

"We're all God's children."

I don't have ready-made answers about what to do for the poor, whom Jesus says will always be with us. Should I have handled that situation differently? Can't say, for sure. It's easy to be cynical about some of the folks I encounter on the streets. Or anywhere else.

But I hope, at the very least, that Barbara's words, or some allegedly random song lyrics, will show up in my head during future encounters—no matter who they're with.

Going for Broke

The company that my friend works for here in town hires a lot of seasonal workers this time of year, and every Monday there's an orientation session for the new hires in the conference room at the office. On a recent Monday, one of the new employees (we'll call him Walter) showed up for his orientation. It was almost immediately clear that he was significantly intoxicated.

First chance they got, the folks from human resources pulled Walter out of the meeting, politely told him that something was obviously troubling him, and sent him home. Whether he was invited back Tuesday was unclear to my friend.

This was, of course, a bit out of the ordinary for a Monday morning and a sensational source of gossip and laughter to company employees up and down the hallway near the conference room. And, to be honest, I laughed pretty hard when my friend told me about it—come on, what kind of person shows up drunk for their first day at a new job?

A broken one, perhaps.

Men and women who understand their own brokenness are often very good at spotting it in others. And so, one employee had a very different reaction. Rhonda, as we'll call her, is a recovering alcoholic herself and watched this scene and its aftermath with a growing sense of discomfort. After Walter had been shown out of the building, it occurred to her that she had an extra copy in her car of a book by the founder of Alcoholics Anonymous and that maybe he could use it.

Figuring that he'd probably be long gone (I might have immediately left the state), Rhonda walked outside the building and had a look around. To her surprise, she spotted Walter

47

not far from the parking lot, smoking a cigarette. A smoker herself, Rhonda lit up one of her own and joined him. A few puffs later, she worked up her nerve and began a very tentative conversation by asking him if he'd been in the orientation upstairs.

Walter admitted that he had, and Rhonda gathered a bit more courage and shared a little of her own struggle. Eventually, she told him about the book in her car and asked if he'd like to have it. He said he would, and waited as Rhonda walked around the building to where she'd parked and returned. She handed him the book, and then Rhonda and Walter went their separate ways.

I wonder which one came away from the encounter feeling more encouraged.

Their paths may never cross again. Walter may be somewhere right now with a bottle in hand, lamenting another botched opportunity. Or maybe not: perhaps Rhonda's kind gesture will help nudge him in a new and different direction. Maybe that Monday morning was his "rock bottom." We won't know the end of the story.

But if Walter ever makes some changes in his life, I'm betting it will be because of a seemingly small act of compassion, someone stepping outside of their own trepidation for a minute, as Rhonda did. I'm also willing to wager that Rhonda's ability to describe herself today as "recovering" is because someone, sensing she was in trouble, once reached out to her.

Compassion is not only a beautiful, life-giving—and potentially life-saving—thing. It may also be the best possible option we have for the way we live and spend our days. Desmond Tutu, the South African archbishop and Nobel Peace Prize winner, says, "I am created in the image of God. I am a God carrier. It's fantastic. I have to be growing in godliness, in caring for the other. I know that each time I have acted compassionately, I have experienced a joy in me that I find in nothing else."

I suspect Rhonda can relate.

It's a Garnish, People!

Years ago, I received a birthday card that asked, on the front, why birthday cakes aren't made from health food. Inside, the answer was something like, "Because health food tastes like [word generally frowned upon in polite circles]."

As is the case with many things that are somewhat unsavory, there's some truth to this. In my culinary experience, very little that qualifies as "good for me" can also be described, in good conscience, as "something I would seriously consider putting in my mouth." Yet many people I know, some with seemingly close-to-average intelligence, regularly force themselves to ingest items that I would call "just a notch or two above roadkill," allegedly because such items are good for them.

It's fun to watch them try to seem cheerful about this.

I've even been present, on more than one occasion, when

someone has voluntarily choked down kale. It's my understanding that God created kale specifically as a garnish, much
like parsley. Parsley, we all know, is only edible if you're interested in having obvious and people-repelling green flecks
caught in your teeth. I'm fairly certain there's not enough
chocolate syrup in the world to make either kale or parsley
palatable as an actual food.

If I ran the world, scenes like this would be commonplace:

Doctor: "Looks like your cholesterol and blood pressure
are up a bit."

Me: "Hmmm. That sounds grim and potentially fatal. What
should I do?"

Doctor: "I'd increase my daily Krispy Kreme intake. That
should get those numbers moving in the right direction. And
a bit more fettucine alfredo would be good, too."

However, as of yet, I don't run the world. Thus, some among
us think it's okay to eat kale.

Others believe raisins are a good thing, too. Whose idea
was this? Essentially, to make a raisin, you take something
perfectly edible on its own, a grape, which is reasonably tasty,
and then heat and dehydrate the bejeebers out of it until it's
tiny, dark, wrinkled, squishy, and disgusting.

I mean, if someone were to suggest doing that to a cheese-
burger or a brownie, you'd think they were, in the words of a
song I once heard, "One fry short of a Happy Meal." I would
not argue with you.

Quinoa is also quite the thing—all the cool restaurants
serve it now. Not really knowing what it was, I consulted my
favorite semi-reliable information source, Wikipedia. There,
I learned that quinoa is "not a grass," which is good. I don't
eat grass. It is, however, a "pseudocereal botanically related
to spinach and amaranth." I immediately noticed "pseudo" in
there, so apparently it's some kind of fake. Also, I have no idea
what "amaranth" is, so I again inquired of Wikipedia, where I
was told, "most of the amaranthus species are summer annual

weeds...commonly referred to as pigweed."

Nope.

Before I left Wikipedia, I also learned that in 2016, China produced some ninety-two percent of the world's spinach. I have actually eaten spinach before and lived to talk about it, albeit somewhat unhappily. However, it seems a bit unpatriotic now.

I suggest that this is a time to show our deepest support for our country. America produces about 1.5 *billion* gallons of ice cream or similar desserts every year, ranking us number one in the world. We also lead the planet in ice cream consumption, with each of us putting away an average of forty-eight pints a year. These are not distinctions we want to give up in our rush to the kale aisle. You know other countries would love to have those trophies.

There is, however, a bright spot in the health food world. Looking to add some iron, fiber, and antioxidants to your person while also, perhaps, lowering both your blood pressure and risk of heart disease?

Dark chocolate. Lots of it.

On Our Own?

I'm about as far from a medical expert as it's possible to be, but it was my professional opinion that the woman on the floor of the restaurant that day was dead. She didn't budge as she lay on her back, and there was absolutely no trace of color left in her face. She was about twenty feet away from the table where two friends and I were eating our lunch, and apparently had suffered some kind of seizure. We didn't see her collapse and by the time we figured out anything was happening, 911 had been called and several people were gathered around her. Even so, as she lay on the hard floor, I remember thinking how alone she looked.

Seeing her there took me back a bunch of years to, oddly, the first time I'd ever been on a plane at night. A college student, I had felt my fledgling faith being shaken on that flight, and it wasn't because I was convinced it was really impossible to find runways in the dark. It was all those lights. As we flew over cities and towns, there were thousands and thousands of lights below me—on houses, office buildings, shopping centers, roadways, and countless other places. How, I wondered, in the immensity of all that, could there possibly be a God who kept track of every one of us? I remember feeling pretty alone in the sky that night.

Being alone might be what we fear most, and living life still has a way of making us feel like sometimes we really are on our own. But, if I can get past those feelings to what I believe is true (a tough leap at times, surely), I can arrive in a place where I don't think either the unconscious woman in the restaurant or the college kid on the airliner was ever really alone, even if neither of us knew it.

One of the names given to Jesus by the prophets is Emmanuel, which means "God with us." God's presence and intimacy with us is an amazingly comforting and inspiring idea, and I wish I could irrefutably demonstrate its truth, both for myself and for everyone around me. I can't. If I could, there would be no need for faith.

I do, however, have these words from a more grown-up Jesus: "Are not two sparrows sold for a penny? Yet not one of them will fall to the ground outside your Father's care. And even the very hairs of your head are all numbered. So don't be afraid; you are worth more than many sparrows." And later, "Be sure of this: I am with you always, even to the end of the age."

I'm not sure we can accept those kinds of words until we actually try trusting and living them. When I can let myself do that, I sure do like knowing that I'm never outside of God's care and presence, and that he knows the number of hairs on my head.

In the times when the prophets first called Jesus Emmanuel, names often came loaded with more meaning than they do today. "By calling God Emmanuel, we recognize that God is committed to live in solidarity with us," says writer and priest Henri Nouwen, "to share our joys and pains, to defend and protect us, and to suffer all of life with us. God-with-us is a close God."

The woman on the restaurant floor, fortunately, proved my lack of medical expertise by reviving, and she was speaking with EMTs when I left. But even if she hadn't, I'd still believe that God was closer to her than I'll ever know.

I believe that because Jesus said it's so. And I love the way the monk Thomas Merton puts it: "Whether you understand it or not, God loves you, is present in you, lives in you, dwells in you, calls you, saves you and offers you an understanding and compassion which are like nothing you have ever found in a book or heard in a sermon."

We ain't flying solo.

You Talking to Me?

When I was a kid, I was a big fan of the spy-spoof TV show *Get Smart*, which made great sport of the cloak-and-dagger world of espionage. Whenever the hero, Agent Maxwell Smart, needed to have a top-secret conversation, the "cone of silence" would descend around him and whomever he was talking to in order to protect their privacy. It was awkward, especially the portable version, and enormously ineffective.

I thought of the cone of silence recently because I'm convinced that most people walking around talking on their cell phones in public believe they have one and that it really works.

They don't, and it doesn't.

I had started, for example, to think that many of the customers in my local grocery store were, well, lunatics. They walked up and down aisles gesturing and having lengthy, animated conversations with, from all appearances, themselves. Eventually, it dawned on me that these people were actually ahead of me on the technological curve and were just using cool earpiece phones. Still, sometimes I think people conversing on their Bluetooth gizmos (Blueteeth?) in Aisle 4 are talking to me, but when I attempt to join the conversation, they make me feel like an intruder. It hurts my feelings.

I'm pretty sure when the muttering undead of the Zombie Apocalypse roll in, I'll be oblivious: I'll assume it's just those guys I saw in the produce section.

Many folks who apparently have been deemed capable of carrying cell phones also take the "public" in public transportation entirely too seriously. My oldest daughter caught the MegaBus home for a weekend from college once. The ticket was a good deal, and, at no extra charge, it included the appealing ambiance of a woman a few seats away sharing with passengers, in rather excruciating detail, an unfortunate rash she was currently dealing with.

"I'm pretty clear that the rash was 'red and bumpy,'" my daughter reports.

I was once on a train a few seats away from a young woman who spent most of South Carolina discussing the ups and downs of her relationship, evidently with the other participant in the alleged relationship. At times, things seemed to be going rather well; at other times, the rest of us were treated to a demonstration of the so-called thin line between love and hate.

My favorite part of the conversation: "Now that you're divorced, are you ready to work on being my man?" Pause. "No, you should NOT have to think about that!"

The nearly two-hour chat ended with "Love you"—and a seemingly complete lack of concern that a bunch of train passengers now knew almost as much about her life as the guy on the other end of the phone did.

I will admit, however, to having been on the other side of this important issue, too. On another train trip, I found myself in one of Amtrak's "quiet cars," in which passengers are only supposed to whisper and cell phone conversations are verboten. Not being fully aware of the rules, I got a phone call and had a brief and—I thought—rather quiet little chat. I glanced around the car just before I hung up and noticed several of my co-riders looking at me like I'd just poked them in the eye with a stick. One was frantically (and somewhat threateningly) pointing me in the direction of another car.

Let's be clear: It's okay when I do it, people. And I never even brought up my rash.

No Pedestals Required

A friend of mine once attended a funeral where, during a moment of prayer, the minister looked out over the gathered mourners and solemnly intoned, "We thank you, God, for the gift of immorality."

He corrected himself pretty quickly, says my friend.

Another minister, one I know well, meant to close a service with some verses from the New Testament book of Jude. What came out was, "Here are a few words from the book of Dude."

I share these incidents not just because I think they're pretty funny. They also make an often-overlooked point: Men and women who've given their lives and careers to the ministry, despite the expectations we often burden them with, are exactly the same as you and me. While certainly worthy of our respect and gratitude, they're far from perfect—and that's a very good thing.

I grew up putting members of the clergy on very high pedestals, and was told that to become one was one of life's highest aspirations. They lived on a higher plane than I did.

Once, when I was ten or eleven, Sister Gabriel—an old grade-school teacher of my mother's who was probably somewhere in the neighborhood of seventy at the time—came to visit. As we sat in our living room, I worked up my courage and timidly asked her if she was "allowed" to listen to the *Jesus Christ Superstar* album, which was fairly new. I fully expected her to reprimand me for asking, and was astounded when she laughed and told me how much she liked it. A nun who listened to rock music? A whole new world suddenly opened up.

What's next? Does the Pope watch *The Flintstones?*

Today, while we may not have quite the reverence for them that we once did, we still tend to measure men and women of the clergy with a different yardstick than we use for ourselves, and often lose sight of the human being trying to do that job.

And what a job it can be.

Another minister friend once received a late-night phone call and became one of the first people to arrive at the scene of a gory murder-suicide. What do you say to a son as his parents' bodies are being bagged and taken away?

It's not out of the ordinary for a member of the clergy to look up and find a distraught woman in the office doorway, bearing the stricken look of a wife whose husband has just left her. Or to get a phone call from a man who's just lost his job. Or to be called suddenly to the hospital to be with people during the most difficult moments of their lives. Or to be the one who's expected to ensure that the couple's wedding ceremony is a joyous one, or to put the most comforting face possible on at a funeral service.

These kinds of situations must be when the expectations we put on the clergy are hardest to carry, because many people come looking for more than support and guidance. They half-expect that their pastor, rabbi, or whatever can *fix* the situation, somehow say exactly the perfect thing and make them feel all better. Representing God in a tough moment, clergy are supposed to come bearing His full power and comfort.

That's an impossible assignment for anyone, because a lot of stuff is just flat-out unfixable, certainly not immediately and often not in this lifetime.

Ministers don't have a better pipeline to the Almighty than you or I do. Mostly, I think, they spend a lot more time— and make it a much higher priority—keeping that pipeline open and flowing. But they're still you and me, perhaps with a collar.

So, maybe we need to adjust our expectations a bit. Maybe

we should look to the clergy primarily for words of comfort and truth, prayer, and, perhaps most important of all, presence. Maybe the very best thing we can do for each other in times of crisis, clergy or not, is just to be there. And be human together.

I think Sister Gabriel would be all over that.

Did She Just Say What I Thought She Said?

One of the great comedic opportunities of everyday life is overhearing someone, or being overheard, completely out of context. The possibilities are endless.

As my wife and I sat in a restaurant one morning, she announced to me, at the precise moment our waitress happened by, "He didn't sleep with me last night—I really hope he sleeps with me tonight."

The "I don't think I was supposed to hear that," amused-but-quizzical look that appeared on our waitress's face made me laugh so hard I almost choked on my omelet. She didn't realize my wife was talking about our cat, Otis.

Context is everything.

Another time, I passed by just as an irritated woman snapped into her cellphone, "What do you mean, 'Is Kyle still in a coma?' Kyle's never been in a coma!"

I would love to know the context for that one.

I thought about this recently as I tried to understand and appreciate some of the things Jesus said, because without context I often don't do a very good job of either one.

One of his best-known parables is the one about the Good Samaritan. For years, I thought of it as a nice story about an unlikely hero. Then I learned a little about how the Jews Jesus was telling the story to *really* felt about Samaritans. There's a long territorial and historical backdrop, but suffice it to say that most Jews thought Samaritans worshipped God wrong, were unskilled and uneducated, weren't true Israelites, and were likely half-breeds, too. One of the worst insults a first-century Jew could hurl at someone was to call them a Samaritan (which the crowds later did to Jesus himself). Maybe the best analogy I can come up with is how many Americans today feel about members of ISIS and other terrorist groups.

So, Jesus hits the crowd with a story about some very upright priests and ministers who are too busy doing "important" things and won't stop to help a man in distress—but a Samaritan who goes above and beyond to show God's love to a fellow human. The parable had to shock and offend his listeners.

It also underscores the completely radical way Jesus presents faith for his followers, something I often and easily lose in much of what he says and does.

And if accepting and praising a filthy Samaritan wasn't enough, Jesus goes here, too: No one actually enjoys paying taxes, but in Jesus' day it was especially hated because of the people who served as tax collectors. The much-hated occupying Roman forces hired your friends and neighbors to collect your cash, and they made their living by gouging you. The Romans didn't offer a salary and benefits package; tax collectors overcharged you and kept as much of your money as they could. As a result, most of them were wealthy, which further separated them from the general population. They weren't just disliked because they were IRS agents; they were unanimously reviled as traitors, backstabbers, and cheats.

So, Jesus makes a point of having meals with and befriending them and even invites one to join his most intimate band of disciples. Again, this had to be shocking and offensive to most everyone. Many of us have grown up thinking of Jesus as the ultimate nice guy, but "shocking and offensive" was often his M.O., as he made room for society's worst outcasts and forced folks to rethink their lives. It's a hard lesson, both for first-century types and for us.

Just a few days ago, I heard a woman I know telling someone something about "exposing myself." Turns out they were talking about COVID. Context is, indeed, everything.

They Deserve Better

I once had dinner in a restaurant with a local law enforcement officer, and, while we had a great time, what I remember most about that meal is how noticeably uncomfortable he was. He was wearing his uniform, something he almost never does in restaurants, and was very nervous about whether his food might be tampered with in the kitchen because of it.

When in uniform, he said, he only really can relax and enjoy a meal in restaurants where he can see the food being prepared.

He's not a paranoid guy whose imaginary fears are getting the best of him, either. His sentiments are widely shared: "You don't even go through a fast-food window in uniform," another local officer says.

How have we come to this? All police officers do every day is show up for a job that puts their lives at significant risk. They're wherever trouble is, at what is often the worst moments in people's lives, usually standing between those people and life-threatening danger. They're the ones heading for trouble when the rest of us are heading for the hills.

In return, we've made them frequently reluctant to go to public places in uniform. And, even worse, we've made them feel like that uniform, rather than an honor to wear, has made them a target. We've all read about police officers being ambush-attacked in some American cities.

Is it any wonder these officers prefer not to be quoted by name here?

I'm not naive: I understand that there have been numerous incidents of horrible, inexcusable police behavior, at times with racial overtones. I also understand that few of us sign up to be in the kind of situations where life-or-death decisions, made instantly and usually under extreme duress, are part of the job description. It's sure not in mine. And show me a profession free of bad actors and bigotry, or a profession where those types aren't actually an anomaly.

In 2022 in the U.S., 118 police officers lost their lives in the line of duty, according to the FBI, sixty in criminal acts (others died in accidents). That's 118 families who got the phone call they fear every day when their loved one leaves for work.

As they do that work, in addition to its "life on the line" aspect, officers are also often treated with an amazing level of disrespect. A friend who is no longer a police officer remembers having frustrated people scream and swear at her—one man even ran over flares she'd set up—in situations where she'd stopped traffic in order to keep emergency situations up ahead clear of civilians, including one episode involving an active shooter. Her efforts to prevent injury and protect citizens were treated, at best, as a nuisance. As a culture, we seem to have acquired an attitude about police officers.

Sure, it's frustrating if I can't get somewhere as quickly as I'd like, but I haven't, so far, encountered a police officer who stopped traffic because he thought it would be fun to antagonize me that day.

I do, on the other hand, know a state trooper who can tell you what it was like to be at Virginia Tech on April 16, 2007, and the awful days afterward. "There was every shape of badge there," he says, "and that horrific scene hasn't left me or the hundreds of my brothers and sisters in uniform."

As one who generally attempts to obey the law, my experiences with police officers tend to be more like the day I was eating breakfast when my then-high-school-aged son called to report that his car had broken down on the way to school, stranding him, my oldest daughter, and a friend along a nearby interstate.

By the time I arrived, a state trooper had pulled over to

63

help, set up flares, summoned a tow truck, and offered the three of them a ride to school (they declined, knowing I was on the way). The kids, rattled at first by the whole experience, were having a great time.

Okay, that's a nice story and encounters with police officers aren't always jolly conversations. But the men and women who spend their days and nights trying to keep our world running a bit more smoothly are really in the peace and justice business. That's honorable work and they've earned our respect and gratitude—and our prayers.

If Only the Trail Ran Through Here

After listening to my sister's stories about her Georgia-to-Maine adventure on the Appalachian Trail, I'm thinking it might be a good idea for all of us to spend some time on foot in the deep woods. Life on the trail, from what Pat tells me, while hugely demanding both physically and emotionally, seems a lot like life ought to be here in "civilization."

On the trail, everyone is on equal footing, both literally and figuratively. The backcountry is a very accepting place: Pat encountered older people, kids, men, women, and individuals of all varieties of stature, ethnicity, and experience, and almost all of them found the wilderness an excellent place to lower their normal defenses.

"We were all doing the same thing, and we all knew how hard it was," says Pat. "We were all in the same struggle, so everyone was very open to everyone else."

I like the sound of that around town, too.

Economic differences that might have played out back in regular life didn't seem to matter. No matter how padded your wallet was or how spiffy your hiking gear might be, "You couldn't buy your way up the hill," Pat laughs.

On the trail, people are willing to share their stories with one another. Around campfires and among the trees, Pat encountered more than one person fresh out of the military and "walking off the war." She met a woman who was attempting to come to terms with being the victim of a violent crime. She met a man who was hiking as a way to "look for love." (She last saw him hiking with a woman he met as he went.)

She ran into folks who were going through career and life transitions. She met a man who'd made all the fortune he thought he needed and was spending several years traveling the globe in simple ways. She met Boy Scouts and a couple of people who seemed decidedly un-Scout-like.

And she had conversations she wouldn't have had back home in upstate New York. Some of the best stuff of life happens in conversations like that.

On the trail, you can be alone if you want to, but you don't have to be. Pat began her hike with two companions, but they had to drop out somewhere near the halfway point. After that, she went on alone, but almost always met up with hikers heading the same way at about the same speed. Hikers call this their "bubble." There are, almost immediately, no strangers in bubbles and some of Pat's stayed together for weeks at a time.

At night, even the solo hikers would usually congregate around the shelters scattered along the trail, creating evenings of communal campfires and conversation. In the morning, hikers broke camp at their own speed and headed out, only to see many of the same folks that night.

On the trail, there always seems to be someone willing to lend a hand. "If you needed a bandage, some food or water, or just about anything," Pat says, "people would share what they had." Even marijuana, she noted, also quickly noting that she didn't take anyone up on that particular offer.

Information was readily shared, too, as hikers headed both north and south spread the word on what lay ahead. "Word traveled quickly up and down the trail," Pat says. "We knew what kind of conditions to expect and what kind of help and facilities we might expect, even beyond what was in our guidebooks."

On the trail, people understood the importance of rest. About once a week, Pat and her bubble-mates would take a "zero" day, named for the miles they'd cover during those twenty-four hours. It was a time to re-supply and take stock. There were also "nero" days, times of minimal miles to get into a town and settle in for a bit.

Sounds a lot like the idea of the Sabbath to me.

There were also angels on the trail. In hiker world, a "trail angel" is someone who looks out for hikers, often leaving "trail magic" for them. Trail magic can be just about anything, but is often an anonymously-left cooler with treats for hikers passing through. Trail angels also provide transportation into town or to the next day's starting point.

"I came off the trail with a great belief in the goodness of people," Pat says. Her adventure lasted about five months, and it will carry over into the rest of her life.

No matter where we're headed next, I say we lace up our hiking boots.

Ptooey!

There's a retirement community not far from my house and as I drove past it one recent morning, I saw one of the residents out on the sidewalk for a stroll. I noticed her immediately because of the way she carried herself. An elderly woman of Asian descent, she was impeccably dressed, seemingly serene, and walked with great grace. She was just so stately that I remember thinking that for all I knew, she could be a visiting member of the Japanese royal family.

Then, as I pulled away from the light, through my open window I heard her vigorously clear her throat two or three times. I glanced over just in time to see her unceremoniously spit on the sidewalk. After what may have been a hint of a smile, she continued strolling, unruffled.

People are people.

When I stopped laughing, I thought of the Dalai Lama. Strange thought process, I grant you. But here's why: He's a figure revered by millions, sought after for appearances around the globe. At those appearances, he's often given a lavish introduction and a huge ovation—and he wonders why.

"We are the same human beings," he says. "No need for introduction. These people are just like me... If we think we are something special or not special enough, then fear, nervousness, stress and anxiety arise. We are the same."

So, while it may feel a bit strange to consider yourself no different than the Dalai Lama, I think he has a point. To accept it, though, is a struggle because it takes both a certain humility and a certain positive self-image; humility when I'm tempted to think I'm better than that somewhat disheveled, homeless-looking fellow over there, and positivity when

I'm tempted to think that cool, seemingly-together guy over there is better than me.

The truth is, I'm not and he isn't (even if they both feel differently).

Singer and songwriter Matt Maher put it this way in his song *All the People Said Amen*:

"You are not alone if you are lonely
When you feel afraid, you're not the only...
If you're rich or poor, well it don't matter
Weak or strong, you know love is what we're after
We're all broken but we're all in this together."

All of us really do want pretty much the same things, whether our lives reflect it to others or not. We long to be understood, loved, and accepted. We want to feel a measure of meaning in our lives. We'd like to feel that we're accomplishing something. We'd like to be happy and comfortable, but challenged some, too. None of us has quite the control we like to think we do.

And sometimes we'd all feel a lot better if we could just clear our throats for a second.

So why do we spend so much time trying to impress each other?

An interesting part of the answer to that question is that few things get our hackles up more than interacting with someone who clearly thinks they're better than we are. Our relentlessly competitive and celebrity-driven culture promotes a twisted desire to be better, and certainly better-known, than our peers. Go viral and you'll almost surely be happy forever.

I'm tempted to say that this me-first attitude is probably more prevalent than ever today, but I'm not sure there's ever been a time when we've been able to focus more on what's the same about us than what's different. As Maher sings, we're all broken. I haven't met any exceptions to that yet. I don't think it's likely that I will. I wish we could all accept that.

I'd like to spend more time focused on our common-ness than on trying to prove my superiority and correctness. We'll see how it goes. In the meantime, please be careful if you pass me on the sidewalk during my morning stroll.

Airport Follies with Our Fellow Saints and Sinners

If you've ever been through the Atlanta airport, you've probably been on the subway train that zips you from one terminal to another there, and you may remember the computerized woman's voice that so mechanically narrates your ride. Not long ago, my wife and I were on that train, holding onto our overhead straps as Computer Woman cheerfully announced that the doors were about to close. An elderly couple was out on the platform, and they scrambled, hoping to be a step ahead of the doors. But, as we watched, the man slipped on board only to have the doors shut immediately behind him, stranding the woman outside.

Most of us gasped and, as we tried to decide if we should be horrified or amused, the man looked around at us, flashed a huge, only slightly sheepish grin, and announced, "That took me forty-seven years."

As the train pulled away and we all cracked up, his wife stuck her tongue out and gave us all a parting raspberry.

When it comes to people-watching, it's tough to top an airport.

At my first experience with the full-body scanner at Richmond's airport, I pointed to my wedding ring and asked the female TSA agent who was directing me if I needed to remove it.

She fixed me with a stare that felt a lot like a glare and replied, "You men are always trying to take that ring off, aren't you?"

Yikes.

People at airports, travelers and employees both, are experiencing the full gamut of emotions: Some are excited to be going where they're going, some are very stressed, some are exhausted, some are frustrated, many are in a pretty big hurry. And, by the very nature of an airport, they can be from just about anywhere.

Just on the trip from Atlanta to here, we saw a woman in Muslim dress drawing stares as she went through security, harried airline employees who knew that their workday was definitely going to include dealing with angry people, people almost sprinting who appeared not to have run anywhere in a very long time, a weary-looking family with small children—including a baby—trying to make a flight (and you know probably worrying about how loud the kids would be on that flight), and folks dressed anywhere from snappy corporate to beach bum.

Conversations went on around us in several languages; smokers hung out behind the glass wall of the special smoking room, probably feeling a little like they were on display; a man stalked away from an encounter with a gate agent, muttering, "She doesn't know what the [expletive] she's talking about"; and a very upbeat baggage checker called his next customers, a twenty-something couple, to the counter with a loud and hearty, "Come on over, young people!"

We met a cab driver who said he'd waited up to five hours in the airport's taxi lot, in oppressive heat, for his next fare.

He wasn't going to do that anymore and after dropping us off was going back into the city to wait at a hotel instead.

Seatmates on the plane can be interesting, too. My mother once returned to her window seat only to find that the man who'd been in the middle seat was now in her spot, snuggled up against the window and sound asleep.

My college-age daughter once caught a connecting flight, having spent much of the first leg of her trip doing the crossword puzzle in the airline's magazine. Settled into her seat for the second flight, she began flipping through a copy of the same magazine. Without really thinking about it, she passed a little time filling in the crossword puzzle again, this time from memory.

Out of the corner of her eye, my daughter could read her seatmate's text message: "OMG! I'm sitting next to Baby Einstein!"

Maybe she should have given her a raspberry.

"Special" Education, Indeed

I was completely unprepared for the assembly I attended that day at a local elementary school not far from my office. All I knew was that I'd been asked to go by and take a few quick photos at an event.

As students began coming into the combination cafeteria and auditorium, I noticed the first few were in wheelchairs, and assumed staff members were getting some special education students situated before the rest of the youngsters crowded in.

I was wrong.

As I watched, the room filled with more than 100 special education students, guided by their teachers, instructional assistants, and other specialists. The school is one of the public specialty schools in our city, and serves exclusively students with physical and cognitive disabilities, ages 2-21. Its mission, according to Jermaine, the principal, is to "teach our students the functional skills necessary for independent living, and to help them be as productive as possible after they leave here."

It was heartbreaking to look around the room and wonder how possible that goal really was for some of those kids. Some you wouldn't have guessed were special ed students just by looking, others were in various kinds of wheelchairs, and a good portion seemed to have truly profound disabilities.

When I left, I couldn't decide which emotion was stronger—my deep sadness at the seemingly insurmountable obstacles these kids face every day, or the deep appreciation for the amazing commitment and hope shown by special educators every day.

People who work in special education are different than me. One of the first things I did was call Jackie, a retired special ed teacher and principal I know. She listened as I described the assembly, thought for a second, and said, "I can tell that made you sad, but it makes me smile."

One of the teachers at the specialty school, Pam, felt the same way, but it took a while. When she first arrived at her new teaching assignment, she looked around and promptly quit. Her then-principal convinced her to give it two weeks, then the rest of the semester. That was nine years ago, and it's fair to say she's hooked now.

Like most special educators, she's learned to see "can" where most see "cannot," and loves helping make that possible. "These kids face incredible challenges," she says. "Every single day, they get up, get dressed, or have someone help them get dressed, and get ready for school. Just doing that often takes all their strength, all their energy, and all their focus."

What she describes as her students' "heroic efforts to do what others take for granted" leads to progress measured in different ways than for students without disabilities.

"I have a middle school student who's only able to communicate on the level of a two-year-old," Pam says. "What does a two-year-old sometimes do to get your attention? He tugs on your hair. This student will tug on my hair and then say, 'Hi.' That may not be the desired activity, but she's learning to interact."

She points to students who learn to open their lockers, walk a few steps, feed themselves, or make eye contact for the first time. "These kids begin life behind the starting line," she says. "Every inch is a success."

Those inches don't come easy, and the work can be downright hazardous. According to Jackie, "It's not unusual for special ed teachers and paraprofessionals to be hit, bitten, or bruised. And parents can bring their own challenges, depending upon where they are in acceptance of their child's disability and the reasonableness of their expectations. Most disabilities can't be 'fixed,' no matter how badly the parents want us to do that."

And yet, special educators get up and go to school every day, some for decades.

"You have to have compassion for your students and passion for your profession," says Jermaine, the principal. "These students have been marginalized for so long. We strive to do just the opposite here."

"The kids make this so, so worthwhile—just to see the joy, however it's expressed, when they're having fun or mastering a new skill," says Jackie. "We laugh with them, occasionally cry with them, and celebrate with them. There's also so much love between the staff and the kids, and often parents, too."

Some would describe special educators as heroes, but Pam isn't having it. "People will come up to you at the mall and say things like 'Bless you,' but I don't think of it that way," she says. "Our students are just like other kids. When one middle schooler goofs around, they all laugh. The girls look at the boys and the boys look at the girls. We see students as people first, not as people with disabilities."

Real heroes tend to talk that way.

Being and Becoming

The pager in his hand began buzzing before he and his wife even had time to shuffle their way to the booth next to me at Arby's, so she carefully wiped down the table with a napkin while he made his way back to the front for their roast beef sandwiches. I'm not good at guessing people's ages, but I'm thinking they were at least in their eighties, though both appeared to have taken aggressive chemical steps to hang on to the hair colors of their early adulthood. I watched him make his way back with their tray, the weight of their meal seeming to only accentuate his from-the-waist stoop.

Shamelessly, I eavesdropped as I ate and they settled in and unwrapped the goods (don't judge, the place was almost empty and they were right next door). They had an endearing level of comfort and familiarity as they talked about who would call the insurance company in the morning and whether it was best to use the local number or the 800 one.

I tried hard to picture them as twenty- or thirty-somethings, back when they were physically at the top of their game, young and vigorous, maybe a kid or two in tow, and probably not all that concerned with dialing up the insurance guy. I couldn't really come up with a good image in my head (except for the hair color). It can be an odd thing to know someonIt did occur to me, though, that trying to go backward in my head with this couple, while for me perhaps a very natural thought process, is probably (and very fortunately) not God's preferred perspective. From His vantage point in eternity, I think who we're becoming is far more important than who we've been. I'm guessing He's looking ahead. And those of us who try to think with an eternal perspective would probably do well to be doing the same.

Because while I manage to spend an amazingly small amount of time thinking about it, the truth is that everything I say, do, and think every day is a piece of who I'm becoming. Well-known Christian author C.S. Lewis puts it this way: "Every time you make a choice, you are turning the central part of you, the part of you that chooses, into something a little different from what it was before...all your life long you are slowly turning this central thing either into a heavenly creature or into a hellish creature...each of us at each moment is progressing to the one state or the other."

And that "central part," as with most of what's really important about us, doesn't necessarily show on the outside.

Lewis goes on to suggest that the small choices I make today, for good or for bad, lay the foundation for the bigger choices I'll make tomorrow or further down the road, for better or for worse. We're building toward something.

During his travels here, Jesus seemed more concerned with freeing us from our pasts and pointing us toward new and better futures, and more focused on the road ahead than the trail behind. Just three examples: the Samaritan woman with five previous husbands, the rich young man with many possessions, and the woman caught in adultery—He offered all three the chance to erase the past and become who they were made to be. Some took Him up on the offer; others didn't. That choice, and the choices we make each day, have always been ours.

It is a great freedom to know that the one who made us is more interested in who we can and will become than in who we have or haven't been. All the fresh starts we'll ever need are there for the taking. As the book of Lamentations in the Hebrew Bible notes, "His mercies are new every morning."

Lewis, one more time: "There are no ordinary people. You have never talked to a mere mortal...it is immortals we joke with, work with, marry, snub and exploit—immortal horrors or everlasting splendors."

I'd love to be able to think about others that way. Even at Arby's.

A Higher-Stakes Game

Years ago, I watched her ponytail bob up and down as she sprinted down the soccer field, and listened to her carefree giggle as she goofed around on the bench with her teammates on my daughter's team. I chatted with her briefly after games and practices and, at my daughter's request, gave her a ride home a couple times with the carpool. She was fifteen or so, lively, vivacious, and in many ways a typical high school freshman.

And sometime during that soccer season, she thought she was pregnant.

Being fifteen, she had to be naive about so many things, and really had so much further to go before arriving at adulthood than she thought she did. She must have been worried about keeping up with her math homework, fitting in with her classmates, and what she packed for lunch. She probably watched too much television and spent too much time chatting with her friends online.

And she'd been having sex with a boy she knows.

After several anxious weeks, it turned out that she wasn't pregnant after all. And while that meant that there were sighs of relief all around, it's still somehow different when I see her now in her jersey, ponytail, and smile. It breaks my heart, just a little.

No one that I've ever met—hands-off parent, overprotective type, or otherwise—thinks it's a good idea for fifteen-year-old girls to be having sex. And while this girl is probably not guilty of anything other than being young and having an underdeveloped sense of judgment, I can't help but think that she's gone off track, just a little. Anybody that young, male or female, who is sexually active has to have gone off track, at least a little. How did that happen? How does it happen to so many of our young teenagers? Who was supposed to be there for this particular girl when she was making these kinds of decisions, and where were they? What did someone not give this girl that she was seeking instead from that boy? What about him? What did we *all* not give them?

I think of what might have been. If she had been pregnant, she had decided that she was going to have an abortion, and that she wouldn't tell her mother. What's left of her innocence would have disappeared after going through the ordeal of sneaking off to an unfamiliar medical facility to end her accidental pregnancy. She would have had to live not only with that decision, but with the invisible yet solid wall that the secret would have created between her and her mother. That's a lot for a fifteen-year-old girl to bear.

And she wasn't really fifteen anymore. The calendar may have said so, but in reality she was older then. She faced some issues, thought some thoughts, and considered some decisions that she shouldn't have had to until she'd had more time, more experience. Deep down, I think she knew it. Doing research for her book *Fires in the Bathroom: Advice for Teachers from High School Students*, writer Kathleen Cushman interviewed a cross-section of high school freshmen, seeking their advice for their younger peers about making the transition to high school. Here's what one of them said: "Be prepared, just not too prepared. And don't grow up too fast, 'cause once you start hitting your teen years, sometimes you wish you were just little again."

Does this girl wish she was "just little again"? Was she, in fact, a little "too prepared"? Did she emerge from this close call with a revised sense of direction? Did she learn an extremely valuable lesson or walk away feeling like she could take those kinds of risks again? And what did my daughter learn by going through this with her?

It's one of those situations that comes with more questions than answers. I wonder how this girl ended up feeling about herself, and about that boy. I wonder how it made her feel about long-term relationships as she grew older, and what she thought men are like. I wonder if she thought that casual relationships are the norm.

Casual relationships *are* the norm in the hospital unit where my wife worked. It's an intensive care unit for premature infants, and teen mothers are commonplace. Many seem to have a casual attitude about what will be involved in raising their babies, too. I hope this girl didn't end up there. What can we do?

It breaks my heart, just a little.

Getting Up There

A friend of mine can pinpoint the exact moment he realized he was no longer the youthful fellow he still pictured himself to be. He works on a college campus and often gets around by catching rides on the campus bus system. His moment came the day he boarded a crowded bus and, while looking around, had a co-ed offer him her seat.

He told me that story with a chuckle several years ago, and today I'm relating to it better all the time. As I accelerate into my sixties, there are some things I can no longer deny: I draw blanks on people's names, my doctor chats me up about blood pressure medications and colonoscopies, Facebook sends me ads for "hot senior singles" in my area (apparently unconcerned that I have a wife), and, perhaps the greatest indignity of all, a work colleague recently referred to me (in writing!) as a "senior" staffer.

In the face of all this, I needed to get some perspective on this whole aging thing. So, I did what I often do when I need perspective on something—I asked Dad.

I won't tell you what he said about Viagra, but he did say something about the importance of being persistent. Dad's always been very athletic, and today he travels all over the country playing Senior Olympic volleyball. It's given him both a way to stay active and a great sense of community in his retirement.

And he's definitely kept at it. "The key," he says, "is to outlive your opponents." When he and his teammates moved from the seventy-and-over age group to the seventy-five-and-older group, the competition thinned and the medal count grew.

83

"Be careful not to tell the grandkids you only had to beat two teams," he advises.

"Used to be that you heard 'nice shot' or 'nice play,' followed by high-fives; now you're more likely to get 'nice try,' followed by knowing looks or a pat on the head or back," Dad says. "Try to handle these changes with dignity."

Along with the fistful of medals he's acquired, there have also been some of the predictable bumps along Dad's road into his late seventies. "The first body system to change is usually your eyesight," he says, and sure enough, he slips on bifocals as he tackles the daily crosswords and finds night driving a bit more difficult than it once was. However, he hasn't had to resort to cataract surgery yet, unlike, ahem, his son.

"Then hearing becomes more difficult," Dad says, prompting eye rolls from Mom and my siblings, as he's been a bit obstinate about acquiring a hearing aid. We only occasionally resort to near-shouting.

"These changes are all pretty normal," Dad says, "but there can be more, like pacemakers, blood thinners, and new hips or knees." He still has his original-issue joints, but he has undergone bypass surgery and, more recently, began sporting one of those pacemakers. In our family, this may be unavoidable, as I have already acquired my first heart stent. Dad claims to actually be thankful for the family genes, as they've spurred him to stay "reasonably physically fit."

"Aging is a battle," a guy at the gym once told me as he surveyed his growing potbelly, "you can only hope to lose gracefully." But it also comes with some benefits, some of what Dad calls "acquired wisdom." Physical changes can open doors to new areas of the mind and spirit, and a certain sense of acceptance.

I've had the chance to talk with several of my colleagues as they prepared for retirement. I've been struck by the spectrum of emotions that came out during those conversations—some saw even better days ahead, anticipating a new chapter, while others left me sad with their bitterness at unrealized dreams or "unfair" treatment.

I'd like to do this aging thing with a bit of "in-between," both savoring what's ahead and appreciating what's behind. And I'd like to be able to do it with some of the grace Dad's shown. "The bumps in the road almost inevitably catch up with you," he says, "but I'm very grateful for all I have, and how's it's helped me through the tough times."

I'm grateful, too, Dad.

Only Ourselves to Blame

I came across an essay once in which the writer, discussing some controversial issue of the day, described himself as "compassionate and tolerant" and congratulated himself because, he said, when he hears the word "Christian," he doesn't immediately assume anything either good or bad.

Around the same time, I listened to a speaker, a man involved in Christian evangelism around the world. He said that when he applies for admission into a country and says that he's visiting to promote Christian activities, he's often denied entry. But if he says that he's coming to help people be better "followers of Jesus," he's almost invariably granted a visa.

What's going on here? How did the word "Christian," in so many circles, come to have such a sour kind of connotation? Why do so many, when met with a word that's supposed to have so much to do with love and truth, instead feel repelled? And how did "Christian" come to have such political overtones? Why could so many people relate so well to the old "Church Lady" character on Saturday Night Live?

Unfortunately, I think we did it.

By "we," I mean those of us who call ourselves Christians, who say we take our faith seriously and profess to be followers of Jesus. Our self-inflicted wounds are hardly a new development; they've been around for centuries. In fairly recent times, Mahatma Gandhi said of Christianity, "I like their Christ; I don't like their Christians."

It is our failure—those of us who say we are Christians—to live faithfully in response to Jesus' call to love others, not judge them, that has so much potential to send people fleeing in the other direction. Many of us Christians don't do too well at the "not judging" thing, which is why we sometimes find ourselves getting frothy at the mouth over issues that seem, in retrospect, to be beside the point. We've gotten off task. We were meant for so much more.

Like many, I've read the biblical accounts of the life of Jesus, and he didn't seem to be in the condemnation business. To the woman caught committing adultery, after sending her executioners away, he said, "Go and sin no more." He spoke of grace for prodigal sons and searches for lost sheep. He healed those who needed healing, both physically and spiritually, encouraged everyone and loved indiscriminately and unreservedly. Aren't those the sort of things we Christians should be about? Shouldn't we be out there imitating this God-man we say we follow, the one who said what was most important is to "love the Lord your God with all your heart and with all your soul and with all your mind and with all your strength" and to "love your neighbor as yourself"?

A little bit more of that would go a long way.

Instead, what many see and hear from some of us is smug superiority and judgment. Or something like this: A national Christian leader, a widely-respected man whose opinion is valued by millions, was recently asked why he became so involved in a presidential election. This was part of his response: "I had to do everything I could to keep the loony left from capturing the U.S. Supreme Court and shaping its liberal decisions for the next twenty-five years."

I have great respect for that man, but that kind of stuff is not helpful. Why not an answer that talked about his deeply-held convictions and how, as a result of his beliefs, he felt compelled to be involved in the election and lend his support to a particular candidate? What of the biblical admonition, "Let your gentleness be evident to all"?

In his book *Blue Like Jazz*, Donald Miller writes of a Christian group making plans to reach out to a college community during an annual campus festival known for exotic substance use and wild partying. The idea was suggested, facetiously, that the group build a "confession booth" and offer partygoers a chance to confess their sins. A member of the group took the idea and added a catch, one that the group ending up following through on: "We are not actually going to accept confessions," he said. "We are going to confess to them. We are going to confess that, as followers of Jesus, we have not been very loving; we have been bitter, and for that we are sorry. We will apologize for the Crusades, we will apologize for televangelists, we will apologize for neglecting the poor and the lonely, we will ask them to forgive us, and we will tell them that in our selfishness, we have misrepresented Jesus on this campus. We will tell people who come into the booth that Jesus loves them."

Sounds like a good start.

Commission the Statue!

As a former altar boy, I consider myself eminently qualified to speak about all things Catholic. I was a stellar altar boy, too—I knew exactly when I was supposed to ring those bells, and did so vigorously. Yes, I became a Protestant a couple decades ago, but part of me will always follow Papal conclaves almost as carefully as Presidential elections.

So trust me when I tell you I witnessed an actual miracle when I was in the fourth grade. I was a student at St. Joseph's School, outside Nashville, Tennessee, and I was deeply in love with my teacher at the time, Miss Cecilia Baltz. I'm pretty sure she felt the same way, though she never mentioned it. The teacher of the other fourth-grade class was a nun named Sister Terasita. It's true, I swear.

Sister Terasita, tragically, had been born without the ability to crack a smile. Also, according to our best elementary school calculations, she was approximately 154 years old. We just figured she'd always been at St. Joe's and would always be there. She wore the tall head covering nuns wore back in the late 1960s, and a billowing habit that swept all the way to the floor. We never saw her actual feet and weren't convinced she had any, based on the way she just seemed to glide around the school.

She was, um, stern. And she had a paddle.

We lived in abject terror of her, of course, and in complete sympathy with those who ended up in her class, like my older brother. At the other end of the St. Joseph nun scale was Sister Mary Paul, who taught second grade and was beloved by all. We were jealous of anyone who got her as a teacher, like my younger sister.

Miss Baltz's and Sister Terasita's classes often did activities together and, after a while, Miss Baltz didn't even bother to mention to us that we should be on our best behavior on those occasions. We may have only been fourth graders, but we knew trouble when we saw it.

One day, during such a joint activity, Sister Terasita's glide-by down one of the aisles between our desks happened to intersect exactly with the trajectory of a small rubber ball that had been winged across the classroom. This winging was an unprecedented act of bravery and to this day, I'm not sure who the winger was (it wasn't me). What I can tell you is that the ball bounced on the floor next to Sister Terasita and then, to our absolute horror, disappeared under her habit.

Now to the actual miracle: That ball *was never seen again*. Sister Terasita didn't alter her glide or her facial expression one iota. She had no visible reaction whatsoever. She went on with whatever she was doing, in full glide mode, and, I swear, the winger never got the ball back. Those of us fortunate enough to witness this blessed event could only stare at each other in mystified, and somewhat terrified, silence. We were stunned and left to speculate about what else might be lurking in that habit after all of Sister Terasita's years of teaching.

I remain mystified decades later and only a little less terrified. Clearly, this was a full-on miracle and Sister Terasita deserves to have been made a saint by now. I have heard nothing about canonization proceedings. At the very least, she should have a statue. I haven't been to St. Joseph's in a while—maybe they've commissioned one since my last visit. I'd make a contribution toward it—but only if it was sculpted to include feet.

To this day, whenever I see a nun, I think of the miracle at St. Joe's and am tempted to ask the good sister if she's aware of the legend of Saint Sister Terasita. I suspect she is.

When Faith Is
All We've Got

We stood bunched together, staring out the second-story windows across the back of our downtown building, exchanging somewhat guilty glances, but transfixed anyway. How could we not be? The scene below us was somehow riveting and, at the same time, made us want to bolt back into our offices, pretending we'd never seen it.

The accident that had just happened at the intersection at the end of the block behind us had sent one of the cars involved careening into the brick building on the other side of the traffic light. Shattered glass littered the asphalt, and a small puff of smoke rose from the car's crumpled front end, now seemingly fused to the building. A few people were scrambling about, but because we were inside and half a block away, we could hear almost nothing.

Emergency vehicles had begun to arrive, and the professionals took over. Chuck, one of our co-workers a floor below, had heard the crash and run out to the scene. He was back now, and we asked him about the condition of the driver of the car that had hit the building.

Chuck looked back at us grimly. "I think he's dead," he said. We fell silent.

Several long minutes later, we suspected Chuck was right. The EMTs had managed to extricate the driver from behind the wheel, and we watched as he was put on a stretcher, somehow shirtless, and wheeled toward the waiting ambulance, the crew frantically administering chest compressions the whole way.

We felt our suspicions confirmed when the ambulance remained in the roadway, making no attempt at a quick get-away. It had arrived with all haste, siren and lights fully activated, but when it finally drove away, it moved in tragic slow motion, just a rooftop light silently blinking.

The man in the back of that ambulance was not to blame for the crash. The other car had run the red light.

We looked at each other, trying to read stricken thoughts and faces. Almost all of us drive through that intersection every day, and we properly observe the signals of the traffic light, just as this man had done. What an incredible difference one instant, one piece of unfortunate timing, can make. Our illusions of having ultimate control suddenly lay as shattered, at least for the moment, as the windows of the car below us.

I was thinking about a phone call. Someone—perhaps a wife, maybe a girlfriend, a parent or a child—was going to get a phone call soon, a call that would also come unannounced through an intersection in time and change their lives forever. It would be a call they were in no way prepared to answer. And someone, too, would have to make that call.

I thought about the absolute normalcy of it all. The driver of this car was likely on his routine commute home, a drive he'd probably made hundreds of times. He may have been listening to the radio, singing along with a favorite tune or chuckling about some overly-enthusiastic caller on a talk show. Maybe he was preoccupied with thoughts about his family and the coming evening.

And then he was struck, as if by lightning.

Most of the unspoken questions on the second floor were the kind that come without answers. Certainly, this man didn't deserve such a fate. Does anyone? Why him? Why hadn't a car come hurtling in our direction on any of the numerous trips we'd taken through that traffic light? Is fate really that capricious? In the end, how much say do we really have?

I don't know.

I do know that when we left work not long after, my colleagues and I carefully looked both ways as we drove through the intersection. I know we noticed the carefully swept pavement and the spray-painted lines left by the police who came to investigate. I know that we breathed silent sighs of relief when we were safely through the light.

And I know that when we got home, we hugged our loved ones, and we held on a little tighter.

Larry Deserved
Every Salute He Got

The funeral was for a man I barely knew. His name was Larry, and I'd only met him at a few scattered functions in the twenty years since I'd married into the family. But he was Chris's father, and because Chris is my brother-in-law, we wanted to attend the service. I didn't even know Larry well enough to know that he was a veteran. He had served for thirty years in the Coast Guard, and so his burial was held late on a cold January morning at Arlington National Cemetery, in the midst of rolling hills blanketed with the countless rows of gravestones of men and women who served our nation.

There, with almost excruciating formality, the flag over the casket was folded, following a 21-gun salute and a lone trumpeter sounding taps, and presented to Larry's widow by a Coast Guard officer, who spent several moments whispering his condolences to her.

The military has never really been a part of my life in any direct way. My father was in the Army when I was born, but his two years were up not too long after. I hit draft age after Vietnam and after our armed forces had gone all-volunteer. I never considered joining after high school and, like all my friends, went on to college.

As a result, I've always taken our soldiers and sailors for granted.

But as I watched those guards and officers at the funeral, one thing was apparent: Nothing more important to them, in that chill breeze, than seeing to it that Larry got the honor and respect he'd earned in his years as a search-and-rescue helicopter pilot. Those young men and women knew

Larry even less than I did, but their regard for him was evident in every movement.

There was ritual, there was ceremony, there was tradition—but in the end, it wasn't about that. It was about Larry, who, like so many other servicemen and women, had sacrificed for all of us and performed irreplaceable service. And it was about more than Larry, too. It was about the military, and the unbreakable bonds that exist among the men and women who've been a part of it. It was about things that only they really understand.

And it was about us. It was about all of us knowing, as the photos of American casualties that occasionally run in papers and magazines remind us, that real people are involved when military activities take place. People who may have a spouse who sat at the gravesite, or children to watch the flag be folded. In Larry's case, there were also grandchildren, some of whom were saying their first final goodbyes to someone. In many cases, there are also parents left to cope with the unfathomable loss of a child taken far too young.

Those tragedies, those feelings, and those ceremonies are going on right now, and they're happening no matter what we might think of our military's current activities overseas. Politics aside, the war there has been going on for several years now and, for me and many like me who don't feel a direct connection to any current serviceman or woman, it has often become just another report when we're checking the news. News anchors aren't broadcasting live from Afghanistan much anymore, and the war slips away, losing its sense of urgency and immediacy. It feels like there's still a long road ahead, with no resolution in sight. Signs of progress are hard to come by. And so we get bored with it.

That makes it easy to gloss over the raw realities of what's happening. Larry didn't die in combat, but his funeral reminded me that somebody's children *are* doing so, right now. Their families are receiving those painstakingly-folded flags and going home to empty rooms and irreversibly altered lives. I can't overlook that, as I live my life in freedom.

Thanks for all you did, Larry. Rest in peace.

Doing Lunch

A few years back, DeAndre and I got together for lunch every other Tuesday in the cafeteria of his downtown elementary school next to a housing project. He was seven, a semi-enthusiastic first grader, and my "lunch buddy."

The idea of the lunch buddy program was that maybe men and women from the community would have something to offer to at-risk kids growing up in tough neighborhoods.

And DeAndre was definitely at risk. I knew that, though there was an awful lot about him I couldn't begin to know.

I knew where he lived, because one day he invited me to come to his house, scribbling down an address on a scrap of paper. My heart sank when he handed it to me; the street was one I'd occasionally hear mentioned on the news, and not for its hip gentrification or beautification projects. I hoped and prayed that as he grew older he'd be able to keep himself off the news.

Eventually, I met his mother, a very sweet woman who seemed very determined to keep him out of trouble. DeAndre (not his real name) said he has two brothers in their twenties, one of whom was in jail because "he had a fight." He also said his father lived with his mother and him, so, unlike many of his peers, he came from a two-parent home. Another tidbit about his father, though: "He doesn't like white people."

Still, someone from home had signed the form giving DeAndre's school permission for him to have a lunch buddy.

I don't know what kind of impact his father's statement about white people has had on DeAndre. I didn't see any white students during our lunches in the cafeteria, and only a couple of white staff members at the school. He later visited our home several times, loving our little dog more than I did and discovering that he and my youngest daughter knew most of the same lyrics to Rihanna songs. Does he think all white people live in relative comfort and safety? I know he looked at our neighborhood with yearning when we rode bikes or walked the dog there, and he frequently asked if he could stay overnight.

I don't know, either, how seriously to take a lot of what DeAndre told me. For instance, he said he had both a PlayStation 2 and an Xbox and plenty of games for them, and that he spent one spring break in Florida, Maryland, *and* New Jersey, so I was often a little dubious.

The passage of time has left a lot of things about DeAndre unknown to me now. We lunched together until he finished fifth grade and moved on to middle school, where it was considerably less cool to have a lunch buddy. We kept in touch much more sporadically after that, eventually losing touch altogether. He'd now be finished with high school.

I'm not naive enough to think that occasional lunches and visits with my family revolutionized DeAndre's life. He faces huge challenges. I hope we helped expand his horizons a little, taking him to see our son at college and for a hike along the York River. (His question upon seeing it: "Is that the ocean?")

I hope we gave him a more balanced view of white people. In an e-mail, his mother once said, "You and your family have shown him that no matter what race, there is such a thing as friendship."

I don't know much about where DeAndre's future will take him. I'm hoping he still has his youthful exuberance; I'm not sure how much youthful innocence is left.

One day when he was around fourth grade, I asked him what he hoped to be when he grew up.

"I want to be a pimp," he said enthusiastically.

I asked if he knew what that meant.

"A gangster," he replied, grinning.

I wish I knew how much hope to have for him. I want to believe he can escape his neighborhood, or somehow help change it. I want to be optimistic for who he'll be years down the road; that he'll have a family, the kind with a spouse you love and children you're there for. I want to hope that he'll have a job, a career he feels good about. I want to hope that he'll feel a part of a community he's happy to call home. I want him to have dreams, and to be safe.

Godspeed, DeAndre.

The Female of the Species?

I've been around women all my life. There was at least one present at my birth; then, in one of the great practical jokes of all time, my parents went on to provide me with four sisters in subsequent births. These days, I have a wife and two daughters. While I do also have a brother and a son, I've spent big chunks of my life knee-deep in estrogen. And yet I know so little.

All this to say: What planet do the women in some of those Super Bowl ads come from?

Just a couple examples: I've eaten fast food for a lot of years, but I've never seen a woman eat a burger the way the woman in the burger joint commercial ate hers. Apparently, to her, eating is an excellent way of attempting to seduce any man who might be passing within a fifty-foot radius. (Okay, technically it was a cod sandwich, and she was consuming it on a beach, but you get my drift. Frankly, I'm not sure which is less realistic—the way she ate the sandwich or the fact that someone really eats cod sandwiches.)

The two lead actresses in a sitcom chose to draw some attention to their program with a round of pole dancing and various other forms of writhing. I recall being closely involved in the entire dating process with my wife and, though I've thought about it a lot, I don't remember her doing any actual pole dancing.

To test the theory that finding all this strange and unnecessary only proves that I'm out of step with the times, I called my older daughter, who was away at college, and asked her if she'd ever employed pole dancing as a dating strategy, or for any other purpose. "I have enough trouble not running into poles," she said.

Somewhat reassured, I called my younger daughter, who was also away at college and lives in a dorm right across the street from a fast-food burger joint. "Have you ever gone over there and eaten a burger the way the woman in the commercial did?" I asked.

"Only every day of my life," she replied, then quickly retreated. "If she eats a lot of fast food, no matter how she does it, she wouldn't be that skinny."

I felt a little better, both about my daughters and about life in general.

We all know what ads like these are about: they're about women blatantly flaunting their bodies to sell products, advance their careers, and titillate viewers. And we seem to play along willingly. I know that members of both genders regularly flaunt their bodies in the real world, too, but I'm wondering: Do the women portrayed in any of these Super Bowl ads actually exist anywhere? If they do, I haven't met them. Granted, I don't get out much.

But the woman I married and the women I've grown up with, tried to be a decent father to, worked with, and lived in the neighborhood with have pretty much been like me—just trying to make some sense out of life and looking to love and be loved. Seems they're actual humans, and rather strongly opposed to the idea of being seen as objects for the gratification of men.

I get that, and I respect it. Does that make me a prude? If so, I can live with that. I'm thinking we could use a few more prudish advertising executives.

I'm just a guy trying to live what I say I believe, and frequently not succeeding. Ads like these are destructive—for everyone. Here's something I know: In a culture that didn't value women, Jesus treated every woman he met with respect, even when the world wouldn't have expected him to. He was kind to the Samaritan woman who had had five husbands and was then living with a man who was not one of them, and he defended the reputed prostitute who publicly bathed his feet in oil.

He also said, "Blessed are the pure in heart."

I have a hard time picturing him enjoying some of the ads shown during the Super Bowl—or not being saddened that so many impressionable young people, and increasingly jaded older ones, saw them.

What's Good for the Goose Ain't Necessarily Good for the Gander

Some years back, before I knew downtown Richmond very well, I drove down Third Street and hung a left on Main. No big deal, except that Main is one-way—to the right. It took about a half-block for this to dawn on me, thanks to the helpful horns and gestures of correctly-facing drivers, and I was able to escape unharmed into a small parking lot. I've now worked downtown for twenty-something years, and only go the wrong way occasionally.

This behind-the-wheel faux pas came to mind just the other day as I headed (correctly) down a different stretch of Main, only to be confronted by a car coming toward me. Fortunately, it was in the other lane, so I had time to offer a helpful horn of my own. The driver went by, still seemingly oblivious, but was quickly flagged down by a pedestrian and set straight before any harm was done.

"Jeez—what a terrible driver!" I thought, a tad disconcerted. "She could have killed us both!"

When I finished muttering, it occurred to me that when I went the wrong way on Main way back when, it was a semi-comical but harmless misadventure. When this woman did it, it was a dumb, life-threatening blunder. It hadn't crossed my mind that I, fine driver and human that I am, could also have killed someone.

What a double standard I'm capable of walking around with.

Lots of us have this amazing ability to rationalize and make light of something we've done or said, but aren't nearly as quick to cut others the same slack. It's a skill that develops when you spend too much time walking around thinking of yourself as the focal point of your own personal universe.

I don't completely hog the double standard, either; it extends to people I know and like, too. An elderly friend of mine thought he'd left his sunglasses at a restaurant one day, so I drove him back and he went in to check the lost-and-found. He came out looking way better than when he went in, sporting a slick pair of shades.

"Find 'em?" I asked.

"Close enough," he replied with a wide grin.

I grinned back, also greatly amused. Yeah, he'd swiped someone else's left-behind sunglasses, but it *was* funny.

When I think about it, though, I realize what I'm really doing when I apply the double standard is saying that people I approve of—and, mostly, me—are better than everyone else; that we can do and say things others shouldn't. That's a pretty good working definition of arrogance.

There's a lot in our culture that says arrogance has its advantages, but as is so often the case, my faith has an entirely different message. The apostle Paul, writing to the growing church in Philippi, a city in Greece, said, "Be humble, thinking of others as better than yourselves. Don't look out only for your own interests, but take an interest in others, too."

While that may seem rather obvious, how many of us make it a priority as we wander through our days?

Jesus tells the story of a man who arrived at a banquet and decided to grab one of the seats of honor, perhaps at the head table, only to be greatly embarrassed when the host showed someone else to that seat, sending the first man off to the back somewhere.

There are a lot of definitions for humility, but one I've always liked has to do with not going around comparing yourself to others, always looking for a reason to be the winner in that comparison. That will almost always become an unhealthy and alienating obsession. As the lyrics to a song I really like say, "My thirst for myself left me wanting more."

The woman driving the car the wrong way and coming at me on Main was probably every bit as unfamiliar with Richmond as I was when I did the same thing. I'm delighted that both of us were stopped before we did any real damage.

My faith tells me that an awful lot of grace has been extended to me, and so I hope to do better at extending it to others. They deserve it every bit as much as I do.

The Truth Will Set You Free. It May Also Make You Very Queasy.

I've become a big fan of pharmaceutical commercials. In a typical thirty-second spot, there seems to be *just* enough time for the narrator to get the name of medication out before launching into a long and deeply unsettling list of the potential side effects you may have to endure if you actually take it.

With some of these products, you may feel better—but you'll almost certainly suffer publicly humiliating gastrointestinal symptoms, develop male pattern baldness, or put on several hundred pounds. Some of your organs might, technically, explode.

After taking the medication for a while, you may fervently wish for death, which, fortunately, is another of the possible side effects. If you listen to the commercial carefully, you can pick up on the fact that the spokesperson is not only trying to run through the list of side effects with record-breaking speed, but also sometimes in Latin.

Clearly, pharmaceutical companies only list the possible effects now because the law says they must. But I think it's so helpful—and entertaining—that we shouldn't just require it for medical products. Lots of companies could be doing so much more to keep us potential consumers better informed.

As you browse at the car dealership, for example, the salesperson should tell you, "I'm required by Congress to inform you that fueling and maintenance of this Saskatchewan SUV will be roughly the financial equivalent of having two extra children in private school. Also, the sticker price is such that you may have to trade in one of your actual children, preferably one with low mileage, to get it. On the other hand, this baby has a mega-sonic and completely epic stereo system. [Pause] But I must also tell you that listening to anything above volume level four will result in near-total hearing loss two years before your payments run out. So, what's it going to take to get you to drive this home today?"

Now we're talking.

There are lots of places this can go. Whenever a reality show appears on your TV, it should be accompanied by a required message on a crawl across the bottom of the screen: "You know they're making this up, right? I mean, c'mon, have you ever seen *real* people act like this? Just to be fair, we should tell you that continued viewing may be harmful to your ability to interact with fellow humans in a coherent way. Here's a list of excellent books you could be reading instead..."

As you browse profiles on an online dating site, photos should come with a blinking message saying something like, "Objects appearing on your screen may be much older and less attractive in real life than they appear here. We also urge the verification of marital status and recommend extreme caution if profile photo seems to be taken in an orange jumpsuit."

When being led to your seat in a restaurant whose health department record you may have reason to suspect, the host/hostess should offer an admissible-in-court update, such as, "We had an amazing power surge overnight and all our 'fresh' meat and seafood is freezer-burned like you can't even imagine. Don't try, by the way. All the turnips and most of the rutabaga look great, though."

Warnings would also be excellent in the strange land of social media. When you sign on, you should get a screen with this: "Do you even *know* these people? Or are following them because you saw them on a reality show? [If this is the case, please go back three paragraphs.] Habitual use of this platform will likely leave you pale, cranky, and annoyingly opinionated, though you may know some great jokes."

It's evident that Big Pharma is on to something, and other

industries should benefit, too.

In closing, federal law says I must inform you that reading this column has made you significantly better-looking, as well as slightly taller. *E pluribus unum.*

Achilles and His Heel

When I was getting started in the publications world and having a spell checker on your computer was still kind of a novel thing, I managed to misspell the word "gauge" in a headline. Not long after, I got a handwritten letter, in perfect cursive penmanship, from a woman who registered her disapproval of this error and went on to question my proofreading skills, my ability to use a dictionary, and, basically, my qualifications for being on the planet. To this day, I get nervous when I use that "g word."

A few years after that, another reader made a copy of a page I'd written and sent it to me, accompanied by a note alerting me to "some weak sentence constructions," all of which were helpfully underlined, with comments penciled in. There were eight examples, according to her, in only five paragraphs of copy. Clearly, I was in the wrong field.

I still have those letters. I'm impressed by the effort both folks went to in those pre-email days. I'm also sure they had my best interests in mind, but I was left, as they say in Social Media World, smh (shaking my head).

"Nowadays people are born to find fault," said Austrian writer Marie von Ebner-Eschenbach. "When they look at Achilles, they see only his heel."

Interestingly, von Ebner-Eschenbach's "nowadays" were almost all spent in the 1800s. A couple hundred years later, we don't seem to be making enormous strides in the fault-finding department.

Speaking of which, what a weird last name Marie had, don't you think? (Oops. Sorry.)

Back to Achilles. In Greek mythology, he was a mighty warrior, a hero of the Trojan War, and the main character of the literary classic *Iliad*, by Homer. He was widely admired for his strength, courage, and loyalty. So, what's the first thing I've always thought of when I hear his name?

The whole heel thing. Why do I do that? Why do we? Is it really just easier to find the negative than to find the good in people and situations?

Perhaps our impulse to find fault in others is, in part, the need most of us have to compete and control, to feel like we have an advantage over people. It's a basic human need to feel noticed, appreciated, even special, but must we denigrate others in order to feel comfortable with ourselves?

When I find myself doing that, I need a reminder that we all stand on equal footing before our Maker and that I, unless I missed the e-mail, have not been given the power to decide who the good guys and the bad guys are. Underneath all the exteriors we put up for the viewing pleasure of those around us, we're all just strugglers on the same path back to the God who made us.

Jesus was offered plenty of opportunities to find fault while he was here, and no one has ever been in a better position to do so. Instead, he forgave, healed, and encouraged.

There's a famous example of how Jesus saw people society had decided were brimming with faults. One day, some religious leaders trying to trap him dragged a woman "caught in the act of adultery" to him and demanded to know whether he supported stoning her, as called for in the law. Before the confrontation was over, he said words that have rung down through the ages since: "Let he who is without sin throw the first stone."

His fault-finding advice for us is very much the same, in an example he once used that must have been almost comical coming from a carpenter. "Why do you look at the speck of sawdust in your brother's eye and pay no attention to the plank in your own eye?" he asked the crowds one day. "First take the plank out of your own eye and then you will see clearly to remove the speck from your brother's eye."

So, these days I'm trying to be more concerned with the lumber blocking my own vision than with what's clouding the eyes of others. It ain't easy. If you see any glaring errors in what I've written here, however, feel free to write. It will be great practice.

God's Gator Gaffe

I recently visited family members in Louisiana and South Carolina. If it were up to me, I would never set foot in either of these states again, and would not be opposed if a movement arose to boot both of out of the Union.

The reason is simple: There are alligators there. Seriously, what was God thinking?

No creature on the planet is as instantly terrifying to me as an alligator. They are smug little prehistoric killing machines. They know it, and they know we know it. Of course, when we happen to see them, they're mostly just lounging around in the mud or in the seemingly-innocent water hazards of pristine golf courses, looking half-asleep and mostly immobile, but that's what they *want* us to think. This is what they're actually thinking: "Sure, I've got these stumpy little legs and I'm several centuries old, but if I wanted to, I could spring up and run faster than your pathetic little four-cylinder Hyundai, which I would also devour as I chomp on you. What's a ton or so of metal to an ugly creature like me?"

This is exactly what goes on in their allegedly small brains. There's been research.

And there's nothing I could do to stop them. Alligator skin is approximately a half-mile thick, harder than diamonds, and impervious to nuclear weapons, which is why they make such excellent shoes and purses.

Speaking of nuclear weapons, this is what I propose: All alligators should be immediately banned from the continental U.S. and rounded up, preferably by those legitimately insane characters on *Swamp People*. Once they're all in custody (the gators, not the Swamp People), they should then be deployed against all international unfriendly types. No nation, armed force, Vladimir Putin, or unruly group of teenagers would stand a chance against a horde of advancing alligators. We could easily rule the world with our battalions of relentless reptiles.

Come to think of it, we'd do pretty well deploying some of the Swamp People, too.

Of course, we'd have a bit of a problem with the gators after they'd finished swallowing up Earth's bad guys. They have insatiable appetites and clearly can't be trusted. They've never made any secret of their desire to dominate the planet, a mission only thinly disguised by their "Don't trouble yourself about me, I'm just barely conscious" attitude.

Not terribly long ago, my daughters were spending an innocent afternoon floating down a river in South Carolina when one of them noticed a gator on the bank. The only thing standing between her and certain, immediate death was a $5 inflatable tube from Walmart. I would have died instantly from eye contact, and I firmly believe every public official in South Carolina should have been arrested before the day was out for allowing my girls within five miles of a gator-containing river. Luckily for said girls, the gator had apparently already stuffed itself with the previous couple hundred tubers, so it chose to ignore them. It probably also had a nasty case of gas, what with all that inner tubing and human pieces-parts working their way through its innards.

According to Wikipedia, the unimpeachable source used by at least millions, "No average lifespan for an alligator has been measured." This is because alligators outlive and/or eat all researchers. I'm told gators just snickered and moved on when the dinosaurs were wiped out. Many of those snickering beasts from back then are still on our golf courses and in our swamps.

And they're watching.

Go Gentle into That Good Day

She's a regular customer at the thrift store our church runs, a retiree who's always friendly and kind when she comes to the cash register with her purchases. One Saturday, she'd bought a couple bulky items that she couldn't carry to her car herself, so we walked out together, both of us loaded down with her latest acquisitions. I noticed the shiny necklace with a variety of sparkling stones she was wearing and asked her about it.

"I got it from my daughter," she said. "She loved to collect jewelry, especially if it was really colorful. She liked those ones the best." She paused, looked at me solemnly, and added, "She was killed in an automobile accident, and I always wear some of her jewelry."

We have no idea of the burdens people around us are carrying.

There's a verse in the Bible, written by the apostle Paul to the people of Philippi, a small city in Macedonia, that I've always liked. "Let your gentleness be evident to all," he told them.

Surely there are times when gentleness may not be the best approach (Jesus overturning and scattering the tables of the money changers in the temple comes to mind), but it's probably a pretty good default setting for us when we encounter one another out in the world.

Another man, I guessed in his fifties, had been in the store several times over the previous couple years, always pushing a woman in a wheelchair and patiently showing her items on the shelves. She appeared older than him and was clearly suffering from some kind of dementia, and I assumed she was his mother. He came in again one day, shopping on his own this time. Before he left, he told me the woman in the wheelchair had died a couple months previously. She was actually his wife; the ravages of Alzheimer's had made her look older.

Let your gentleness be evident to all.

There are several family groups who approach the register and have their children, some younger than ten, handle transactions because the parents speak little or no English. I wonder what it must feel like to be a little kid with the responsibility of communicating for your parents in a new country.

Let your gentleness be evident to all.

I've encountered customers who were shopping for household items because they'd lost their own in a fire; a woman who recognized her own dishes on our shelves, which her ex-husband had taken after their divorce; men and women facing imminent surgeries or biopsies; sons and daughters buying comfortable clothes for elderly parents recently moved into nursing homes; and people donating goods after cleaning out the home of a deceased family member.

Let your gentleness be evident to all.

I've also encountered a woman who plopped a bra down on the counter and asked me if I thought it would fit her, and another who seemed to want me to count the pieces in a 1,000-piece jigsaw puzzle to be sure they were all there.

Let your gentleness be evident to all.

Back in the 1980s, I was hooked on a TV show about police officers called Hill Street Blues. Every episode began with a general roll call and meeting before the officers hit the street, always concluding with the officer in charge reminding them, "Let's be careful out there."

Let's be gentle out there.

I'd Rather Not Share the Road with You

I got angry during my drive home from work the other day, really steamed. I hardly ever do that, but the young woman driving the car right behind me seemed out to injure me—and was oblivious to it.

She wasn't part of an all-out, deliberate plot, but that didn't make it any less true.

She was behind the wheel of a pretty little blue Mazda and I'm thinking she must have had a pretty little phone, too, because she was very much focused on it, to the exclusion of just about everything else around her. Traffic wasn't bumper-to-bumper—it was actually worse, though, in this particular situation. The cars and trucks around us were moving pretty fast, but there were so many of them on that stretch of interstate that brake lights were going on with some regularity in all three lanes.

If those lights went off in the car in front of me, I didn't see any way that Ms. Smartphone wasn't going to rear-end me. And it wasn't shaping up to be a fender-bender. I suspect our encounter would have been something my little Hyundai, or its driver, would not have looked very good after.

Seems like a lot of twisted metal, blood, guts, first responders, tow trucks, traffic jams, increased insurance costs, and messed-up lives for a text message so very important that it likely ended in "LOL," or a phone call that could have waited until later. I did everything I could to get her attention, but accomplished nothing by glaring through my rear-view mirror or waving. She just wasn't looking.

Anger, of course, is usually tied to fear, and I was mad partly because I was scared about what might be about to happen, and my inability to prevent it. Her seeming lack of awareness or concern about the danger she was creating is also part of what made me angry. She was putting people at risk, perhaps most specifically me at that moment, for no good reason—and no one should do that to another person, especially if there's no good reason for it.

I started this by noting that I don't get angry very often, but it's actually happening more and more on my commutes and other behind-the-wheel times. Ms. Smartphone is far from alone: I routinely encounter people who are maneuvering large and potentially deadly pieces of metal machinery around at high speeds while their attention is occupied by a much smaller piece of machinery, one they're holding in their hands. It's hugely dangerous and hugely unnecessary.

Full disclosure: My hands are not entirely clean in this phone-use-while-driving thing, either. I sometimes answer my phone if it rings when I'm on the road, and some of my best phone conversations can happen behind the wheel. I like to think it's okay to do that because I can keep my eyes on the road and I don't do it in heavy traffic. And I never text behind the wheel. But I'm wondering if I should rethink the whole issue and adopt a policy of "no phone use while driving—period."

A little fuel for that rethinking: Driving while texting is six times more dangerous than driving while intoxicated, says the National Highway Traffic Safety Administration. And, at any given daylight moment in America, some 660,000 drivers are using cell phones or other electronic devices while driving a car, according to the U.S. Department of Transportation.

I'm not excited about sharing the road with any of those folks, IYKWIM. (A text abbreviation for "If you know what I mean." I looked it up.) Because, in the end, YOLO (you only live once). And you should do it with as much consideration as you can for your traveling companions here on Earth.

Where Does Justice Come From?

"No justice, no peace!" has been ringing through our streets here in Richmond, one of the hallmarks of the protests and statue-dismantling happening since the death of George Floyd in Minneapolis, Ahmaud Arbery in Georgia, Breonna Taylor in Louisville, and way too many others.

It's a cry born of desperation—and one that makes perfect sense. Without justice, we won't have peace. And, clearly, everybody wants both those things. Our desire for justice and peace is so strong it's driving us into the streets to demand them. To me, it creates a fundamental question: Why *is* that? Where does such a desire come from?

Why do we all understand justice and peace to be good things?

C.S. Lewis makes an interesting point. "Everyone has heard people quarreling," he writes in his book, *Mere Christianity*. "... They say things like this: 'That's my seat—I was there first' or 'Leave him alone, he isn't doing you any harm.'" What got Lewis' attention is that there seems to be a shared standard among us that one person thinks another person is violating. Something about this situation is not *fair*. And the accused person never says, Lewis notes, something like, "To hell with your standard." No, he or she counters with an argument about why it really *is* fair or why fairness doesn't apply in this particular case.

Does the idea that some things are right—like justice—and others are wrong—like injustice—just appear? How did our unspoken agreement about them end up in our heads and hearts?

For me, the only reasonable explanation is that it was put there by our Creator. We seem to roll out of the womb with a sense of right and wrong—it comes as standard equipment. I haven't heard anyone respond to "No justice, no peace!" by saying anything like, "I'm so over this justice thing—nobody really cares about that."

That's because we know it's not true. I think I knew that, even as an eight-year-old living outside of Nashville in the late 1960s. That's when our next-door neighbors, the ones with the George Wallace bumper stickers on all their cars, seared the first memory of racism into my head. When Dr. Martin Luther King, Jr. was assassinated a couple hundred miles down the interstate in Memphis, their reaction was not one of horror and sympathy, but something leaning toward celebratory, and was exhibited all the way down to their youngest son, who was my age. I remember being mostly confused by their reaction, and feeling that something wasn't right.

I believe we're all born with some sense of justice. We know it's a good thing, for everybody. So many things, though, can bury or skew that knowledge within us, like really bad guidance from others, as in the case of my Tennessee next-door buddy.

If we get an inborn sense of right and wrong from our Creator, all that really should be left is getting together and figuring out how to make justice happen for all of us, even if that means sacrifice for some. But, being humans, we find ways to ditch that Creator when we think it's helpful to do so. The biblical prophet Isaiah says, "All of us, like sheep, have strayed away. We have left God's paths to follow our own." For some, our own paths have led to places like this: "Justice, like many other things, is a pretty cool thing, and if I have to get it at the expense of others *not* getting it, that's a deal I'm willing to make."

It wasn't, however, a deal Jesus was willing to make. In the face of some of the injustices of his time, he did things like create a huge public scene by overturning the tables of the money changers at the temple and driving away the animals for sale as sacrifices. He used hated outcasts, like the Samaritans, to illustrate the kind of life he was calling people to live. He stood up publicly to leaders who were abusing their positions. He defended the poor.

Many folks have a picture in their heads of Jesus as a kindly fellow in a robe and sandals who mostly handed out flowers to children. There was some of that, I think, but there was also very definitely a determined defender of the downtrodden and a sworn enemy of all that was evil. Isaiah also described Jesus this way: "He will proclaim justice to the nations."

The section of Lewis' book referenced above is titled, "Right and Wrong as a Clue to the Meaning of the Universe." Hmm. Who's behind this life we all live?

No God, no justice.

The "Hollow" Truth

I mostly remember two things from my high school biology class several decades ago. One was that I was deeply in love with Arlene, a fellow sophomore who was also in the class. Alas, my love was unrequited; she broke my fifteen-year-old heart by asking one of my best friends to the Sadie Hawkins dance.

The second thing is the project we did late in the school year called the Vertebrate Study. We had to write a fairly lengthy report on backboned creatures and on the day we turned it in, we were handed a test to gauge what we'd learned from our extensive, pre-internet research. I can't tell you how many questions there were on that test because I only remember one: Birds are able to fly more easily because their bones are [blank]. This was not a fact I'd turned up in my research and I had no idea how to fill in that blank, so I put some spectacularly incorrect answer.

I will know until my dying day, however, that the bones of birds are hollow.

We really do learn from our mistakes. (Well, most of us do. I'm not sure Arlene did.) Our miscues have a way of lodging firmly in our memory.

Maybe that's why God seems to revel in using our frequently misguided efforts for good, to teach us some of life's most important lessons. It's so in character for him to take something we've done wrong and use it to make us wiser and more faithful than we were before.

It's all grace.

I've made, at last count, approximately a zillion mistakes

way more serious than the hollow bones thing, and I have a tendency, at times, to think God must be pretty disgusted with me for all that. Lucky for me, and for all of us, he's never thought the way I do. Maybe it's that whole "my ways are higher than your ways" thing. His ways are certainly kinder and more patient than mine.

I can cite, for instance, some amazingly inappropriate things that have come out of my mouth at times when I've spoken before thinking about it. Some of these episodes are probably where the expression "cringe-worthy" originated.

When I've consulted with my Maker about episodes like those afterward, I like to think he's revealed to me not just the errors of my ways but how I might use a more thoughtful, considerate way to communicate in the future.

I've rushed through events, conversations, tasks, days— all kinds of things, blundering past opportunities that might have been special moments or chances to do my best work.

As I've mulled those times, I'd like to think that God's shown me a slower, more present, and deliberate approach to the days he's given me now.

I've made snap judgments about people and situations many, many times, only to discover repeatedly that person was totally different than I thought or that something very different than I believed to be happening was really happening.

Looking back, I'd like to think that God has used those moments to speak to me about a slower, more present, and grounded way to go about my life.

Spiritual writer Henri Nouwen suggests that we look at our lives with gratitude—the entirety of them. "True gratitude embraces all of life," he says. "The good and the bad, the joyful and the painful, the holy and the not-so-holy. We do this because we become of aware of God's life, God's presence in the middle of all that happens."

Later, he adds, "Everything that happens is part of our way to the house of the Father."

That's a very redemptive perspective, something else so characteristic of our God. So, despite my life's wrong turns, I'm working on being grateful for what God has shown me as I live them and relying on his forgiveness when my mistakes cause others pain.

I think of that sometimes when I see birds soaring by, no longer earthbound thanks to their strong, light, and hollow bones.

A Guy's Gotta
Have Friends...

I know at least five people who have over 3,000 friends on Facebook. Knowing that I am among their top 3,000 most favorite humans makes me feel rather special. (There *are* billions of us, you know.) It also makes me feel like a total loser. I don't have anywhere close to 3,000 friends—Facebook, imaginary, or otherwise. This is a huge bummer; having spent decades thinking of myself as a massively, wildly popular fellow, my research is showing that I may, in truth, be an outcast.

Welcome to life in Pariah Town.

Not being one to take this sort of revelation lying down, I decided to up my game and begin amassing the kind of friend count more worthy of a guy like myself. The way forward was obvious—because Facebook seems to be hugely successful as a method of friend acquisition, I thought I'd use the strategies I've seen work so amazingly online in actual, well, life.

I began, one fine morning, by taking what I thought was a very artsy, well-composed photo of the brown sugar cinnamon Pop-Tart (unfrosted) I had for breakfast. Smartphone in hand, I approached a random sample of not-yet-personal-friends on my way to work, proudly showed them the picture, and politely asked if they might "like" it.

What I got was a surprising lack of Pop-Tart appreciation, along with some very unfriendly comments about topics such as my choice of brown sugar cinnamon, the lack of frosting, and mostly, um, me. People seemed to be misreading my warm and friendly intentions, and, if anything, my friend count would have gone down if I'd known any of them. Fortunately,

I did not—a fact about which many of them seemed rather relieved.

I went into this having heard a lot about something called "the kindness of strangers" but I'm not sure that's entirely accurate. Some of the people I chatted with seemed a little hostile and not nearly as interested in making friends as I was.

A change of friend-gathering tactics was in order. Maybe, instead of trying to get people to like things about me, I theorized, I should like things about them. So, at a restaurant a few days later, I made a point of stopping by several tables and telling people how much I approved of their tasteful meal choices, being sure to add an enthusiastic thumbs-up gesture each time. In a couple cases, I even threw in some compliments about their clothes and general appearance.

I also mentioned to several individuals in other places how much I liked their cars and offered some the opportunity to see kitten videos on my phone.

Once again, people seemed somewhat less than receptive, with several wondering aloud about the presence of restaurant security personnel. By my estimate, though, I think I came out of that phase of my program with four potential friends (kitten videos are almost foolproof).

Another strategy: Facebook is big on letting you know if you and someone you already know have any mutual friends. Richmond is not an enormous city, so I figured if I approached people who seemed like promising friend candidates and began bringing up some of my friends, instant connections would be formed.

I was met with mostly blank stares, and a few more mentions of security, so I went for mutual hobbies. Mutual exotic places we may have visited. Mutual dentists. Increasingly desperate, I went for mutual diseases, injuries, and surgeries. Mutual defense attorneys. Mutual Kardashians.

I have no idea why Facebook is so popular. In my experience, people respond very poorly to it. Good thing we have a

God whose friendship can handle whatever lousy tactics we might use.

Facebook friends, I've decided, are way overrated. What I really need are Twitter followers.

Slipping Myself a Chill Pill

I don't typically get into conspiracy theories, especially para-noid ones. However, there appears to have been a significant holiday not long ago cooked up by others and celebrated com-pletely without my knowledge. Apparently, it was National Pull Out in Front of Tom Tuesday, and numerous people in the know enthusiastically observed it during my morning com-mute.

As I innocently drove to the office, a succession of drivers decided that there were obvious, wide open spaces in front of my car and seized the opportunity to mosey out of their side streets into my lane, seemingly oblivious to the screech of my brakes. It was so unreasonable the first time or two that I had to laugh, but by the time I got to work, I was actually some-where close to fuming.

It reminded me of an earlier—perhaps only regional—occa-sion when I cruised up to an ATM for what I thought would be a quick transaction. I got this idea because there was only one car ahead of me, and the woman driving seemed to be quite ATM-savvy. I heard lots of beeps as she diligently tapped the screen, leading to the ATM spitting out her card in a timely fashion. I smiled and prepared for her to move on.

Instead, she re-inserted the card and the tapping and beep-ing began again, a process that repeated itself several times as I attempted not to glare from behind my wheel. As I began a short deep-breathing exercise, she literally got out of her car, walked around in front of mine, opened her trunk, and spent a couple more minutes rummaging around in it for something she couldn't seem to find and must have needed desperately.

I hit the gas, pulled around her, and, if it's possible to do this while driving, stormed off.

Why the dramatic jump in blood pressure on both those days? As I'm already on medication for this, it was not helpful. Was there really somewhere so important I needed to be that I just couldn't abide the interesting driving and ATM habits of my fellow humans? What, exactly, was the rush?

I seem to have acquired a need for speed, along with just about everyone else I know. Pastor and author John Mark Comer says that we've become accustomed (addicted, really) to fast and easy—but that the best stuff in life is often slow and hard. The apostle Paul, in his celebrated and often-quoted biblical passage about love, begins with "Love is patient..." James, the brother of Jesus, wrote that we should be "quick to listen, slow to speak, and slow to get angry."

It takes time to cultivate a way of being that is slower, more deliberate, thoughtful, and patient. The kind of character I'm hoping to develop doesn't just happen automatically as the years go by. It's a committed pursuit of living by the ideals we say are most important to us. And, I believe, it entails surrender, admitting to God that our efforts alone aren't going to get us there.

When it comes to other people, there's not a lot I can truly be certain of. Maybe the woman at the ATM could have used a hand with whatever she was looking for in the trunk. Maybe the folks cutting into traffic were late for something they were desperate to be on time for. Maybe I need to be more open to what's going on in the lives of those whose paths intersect with mine, even when it's unlikely I'll ever see them again.

Part of the solution seems so simple, as many of the best answers often do. Both the commute on that Tuesday and the wait at the ATM would have felt a lot different if I could get better at easing off life's gas pedal. An old Finnish proverb I stumbled across recently says, "God did not invent hurry."

I think the Finns are on to something.

Hanging with the High-Falutin'

Years ago, we joined a local neighborhood's pool. My wife, Cathy, was chilling in one of the lounge chairs there one day and got into a conversation with a woman she'd never met sitting in the next chair.

At one point, the other woman asked what neighborhood we lived in. When Cathy told her, the woman responded, "Oh, we know some people who used to live there. They moved up."

I love it when people are pompous. I really do—I think it's kind of hilarious. I'm imagining Pool Lady sniffing a bit as she said that. If I'd been there, I'm pretty sure I would have been unable to squelch my laughter, which I suspect wouldn't have been well-received. (I know, in theory I should feel bad for pompous people and how misguided they must be, and I try to work on that when I'm done laughing.)

Not long after that pool chat, Cathy fielded a phone call from an industrious realtor we also hadn't met who was prospecting for folks interested in selling their homes. During the conversation, he hinted that we surely wouldn't want to be in our "starter home" forever.

The poor fellow didn't understand that our current home was the third one we'd owned during our marriage and was going to be the pinnacle of our real estate acquisitions. Cathy informed him that it was likely she'd "die in this house" and I understand the call ended somewhat awkwardly.

What seemed conspicuously missing in these interactions was any trace of humility, a quality that seems to have fallen from favor in our self-aggrandizing, let's-go-viral culture. Because they see subservience in it, some find the idea of humility a little off-putting, as in, "I really do care about other people and I think it's great to do that, but I'm not getting in line to sign up for something that means de-emphasizing myself, my personality, and my needs."

I think humility is getting a bad rap, though. It's a challenging attribute to define, but the best description of it I've ever heard is that it means not to go around comparing yourself to anyone else. You don't have to lose yourself to do that. You just need, as writer Brennan Manning put it, to "resign as center of the universe."

Here's the thing—and it can be a struggle for many of us to accept: None of us is quite as amazing as we probably think we are, and the rest of the world is not quite as interested in us as we like to think they are (or should be). We're actually just a bunch of humans trying to figure our way through life as best we can, usually while doing our best to look like we've got it all under control.

Here's the other thing: If anyone, ever, had the right to take a pass on humility, it was Jesus. If you believe he was the son of God, then he absolutely could have run the show when he was here, in a place he created. He could have created fireworks and generally left us speechless wherever he went. And he certainly didn't have to end up being executed as a dangerous criminal.

He did end up on that cross, though, because he chose to embrace humility. "The Son of Man came not to be served, but to serve, and to give his life as a ransom for many," is one way he described his earthly approach. It doesn't get much more humble than that. Yet he's the one we remember, the one we base our calendar on.

Turns out it's pretty hard to move up from there.

Flirting with "Miss Amanda"

She had me at "My Dearest," which is how she began her email. Miss Amanda went on to describe herself, not all that humbly, as "a young, lovely, honest, and caring girl." I already had a crush on her.

Seems she was also in a bit of a bind. Apparently, she'd had to flee her native Kenya and was now stuck in a refugee camp somewhere in Burkina Faso. In spite of this, the plucky girl was doing pretty well financially—she had recently inherited $6.7 million from her late father. Sadly, the money was tied up in something called the Islamic Development Bank and only the assistance of a "foreign trustee" like myself could help her get it out. For coming to her aid, I could expect to pocket thirty percent of the cash.

I'm always looking to be helpful, especially for a couple million dollars, so I wrote Miss Amanda and assured her that I was quite willing—eager, even—to be her trusty foreign trustee.

She was delighted and explained in her reply that her father had been tragically killed in a plane crash (she even provided a link to a CNN story about it) and that now her stepmother and uncle were plotting to steal the inheritance from her. Luckily, she said, she had great trust in me, gained from reading my "profile."

Very moved, I seriously considered sending her the information she would need to rescue her money—my name, address, and what I do for a living, along with a couple other items. In the end, I decided not to do so because I'm not, well, stupid. I seriously doubt "Miss Amanda" is any more of a woman than I am or that the sender of the emails even quite knows where Burkina Faso is.

I get these emails a couple times a week, probably because of my international reputation for both generosity and big-money banking transactions. One recent message was especially reassuring, as a "Mr. Baye" noted that "this letter is not a hoax mail and I urge you to treat it serious." I hit the very serious "delete" key, even though he was better off than Miss Amanda—he needed help with $10.5 million and was offering forty percent.

While on the surface these emails would seem to be about as detached from my faith as you can get, when I stop chuckling and think about them, they can actually strengthen it.

Sure, these messages are blatant attempts to play on the sympathy of the naive, using tragedy, injustice, and just plain mean people to relieve folks of large amounts of their money. And sure, they are illegal, immoral, and just plain mean.

The interesting thing is that when we understand that to be true, we're appalled. It's a terrible thing to lie, cheat, and steal. It's just wrong. We all get that. But why? What's the big deal? The answer seems to be there is some universally understood and accepted sense that some things are right and some are just flat-out wrong.

C.S. Lewis put it this way: "Human beings, all over the earth, have this curious idea that they ought to behave in a certain way, and cannot really get rid of it."

Writing in Great Britain during World War II, he added, "What's the sense in saying the enemy was in the wrong unless Right is a real thing which the Nazis at bottom knew as well as we did and ought to have practiced? ... It seems, then, we are forced to believe in a real Right and Wrong."

Of course, we know the Nazis were doing monstrously wrong and evil things. On a much smaller scale, we also know that it's not right for an anonymous someone somewhere with a computer to sell us on the story of "Miss Amanda," tug at our hearts, and make us vulnerable to be victimized. And we know that every day, we do, say, and think things we know, deep down, aren't right.

Think about why.

Subject: FINANCIAL ADVANCEMENT OPPORTUNITY

Hello,

I work with a reputable investment management firm. My Firm mostly represents the interests of wealthy investors who wish to invest their wealth/funds as joint venture or loans into more stable economies and developed nations where they can get good yield and safety of their funds.

Kindly confirm your interest/willingness by a return mail and I will furnish you with details.

Sincerely,

Need People Skills?
Work in a Restaurant.

These days, I spend a lot of time in restaurants. I mean, why wouldn't I? I just lounge around and people bring me food. In my high school and college days, though, life was a bit different—I pretty much only went to restaurants because it was my job.

During my culinary career, I was a dishwasher, cook, busboy, and waiter. I didn't come close to excelling in any of those positions; nevertheless, I still firmly believe that working in a restaurant should be a required part of growing up. Restaurants are one of God's greatest classrooms. I learned a lot of important life skills that continue to serve me today and, to the best of my knowledge, there were no fatalities.

As a dishwasher, for instance, I learned that breakfast should always be served on paper plates because eggs prepared in any way other than scrambled do not come off actual china. Runny eggs cling to plates with the ferocity that fabrics cling to Kim Kardashian.

While a short-order cook, I learned the truth of an old adage my father occasionally used: "Even a blind pig occasionally finds an acorn." My mother hated liver and, as a result, never cooked it at home. I've still never tasted it. One evening, a customer ordered liver and onions while I happened to be on the grill. Trying not to look too closely, I threw a piece of the organ in question on the fire and left it there until I figured it might possibly be edible. I then fried up some onions, plated that sucker, and contemplated leaving early. A few minutes later, however, the waitress returned to the kitchen window to inform me that the gentleman consuming the liver wished to extend his compliments to the chef.

Her news was greeted by the kitchen crew with stunned silence, followed by uproarious laughter. It wasn't the kind of place where compliments were often conveyed to the high school, um, chef.

I also learned that if you're unkind to service personnel, you may live to regret it. After my freshman year of college, I worked as a busboy in the restaurant of a fairly large hotel. In hotel restaurants, you often get the same customers for days at a time because they've got a room a few floors up. One repeat customer, a woman with an unfortunate attitude, had been berating our wait staff for several days, complaining about most everything, and committing the cardinal sin of restaurant dining—tipping poorly.

One day, the beleaguered waitresses threw some of their hard-earned tip money into a pot and offered it to me if I could manage to spill something on her at lunch. So, while diligently refilling her water glass, I oh-so-inadvertently knocked it over with the pitcher. The glass, and a fair amount of water, ended up in her lap. The waitresses were even happier that day than Liver Guy.

Restaurant work also taught me to improvise. I spent another summer as a waiter in a trying-to-be-swanky Italian restaurant, where I opened bottles of wine for customers at their tables. I don't really like wine, almost never drink it, and, to this day, find corkscrews a challenge.

One evening, as my customers looked on expectantly, I broke the cork in their bottle. The top half came out and what was left was significantly lodged further down in the bottle's neck. I eventually asked if I might borrow one of their spoons and used the non-eating end to shove the rest of the cork down into the bottle. However, when pouring the wine, the cork would float back up, block the neck, and reduce the flow of wine to a mere trickle. I poured their glasses, holding the bottle with one hand and using the other to keep the rogue piece of cork at bay with the spoon, then fled quickly.

Nonetheless, I believe restaurant experience is an invaluable part of the growing-up process. You'll learn to think on your feet, and you'll meet all kinds of people. You might even enjoy the liver.

Thus Speaketh the "Innocents"

There's often no predicting what may come out of a kid's mouth—just ask a few teachers.

One year, my friend Barbara, a retired teacher, asked her high school freshman students to tackle a very traditional assignment: write a little about how they spent their summer vacation.

One young man was quite pleased to describe a family event he'd enjoyed attending, writing, "We attended both the wedding and the conception."

I'm guessing that was probably pretty awkward.

Another teacher, who works with high schoolers in Hanover County, was introducing a new concept during an economics lesson and asked her class if anyone knew what the term "distribution" meant. One student piped up quickly. "It's what my cousin went to jail for," he volunteered.

Well, you can't really argue with that.

Teachers sometimes just get to hear the best stuff. It can be the innocent question of a young child: "Ms. Smith, do you work?" or "Did you know President Lincoln?" It can also be a student's honest attempt to answer a question about the Middle Ages by pointing out that numerous people died of the "Blue Bonnet Plague."

At the South Carolina high school where my daughter teaches, faculty members were collecting permission slips from students for an upcoming field trip. A teacher noticed that one young man, when asked to provide an emergency contact, had put "911."

When she questioned him about this, he replied, "I was going to put my aunt, but she wouldn't know what to do in an emergency."

Sounds like impressive foresight to me.

Some students show early promise in specialty career areas, like architecture and plumbing. A kindergarten teacher I know discovered an accidental puddle under the chair of a student and gently asked her what had happened. Glancing upward, the little girl calmly explained that a leak had sprung in the ceiling, but it wasn't a big deal.

"They'll have it fixed by tomorrow," she explained.

A Henrico County teacher was working with fourth graders on a research project about their heritage and family. One boy discovered that his family was of German descent, and was quite surprised. "How can that be?" he asked. "I was born in Florida!"

In his defense, genealogy confuses a lot of people.

An elementary teacher here in Virginia walked by a student who was diligently practicing the cello in the school's auditorium. The little girl was having some difficulty and, seeing a chance to get some assistance, got the teacher's attention and asked if he could "help me with my G string."

After a very serious presentation about how to prevent bullying in an elementary school in the Shenandoah Valley, a group of kindergartners was gathered on the classroom's rug to discuss it. One child immediately raised his hand and declared, "If I saw a bully, I'd hit him."

Clearly, an Old Testament guy.

Our Impressions are "Loaded"

Several years ago, I found myself in need of a handgun. All on the up-and-up, I assure you: I needed it so I could have it photographed for an article I was writing. Since my own expertise with weapons only went as far as some teenage use of a BB gun, I asked around to see if anyone might have a gun for loan.

"Talk to Susan," I was advised by a friend. After I finished laughing and asked again, I was assured that Susan (not her real name) was the one to see.

Susan was a somewhat older, well-dressed, quite dignified, and meticulously coiffed woman who was a mutual friend. In her spare time, she had told me, she liked to figure skate and throw dinner parties. I was quite impressed with the skating and noted that she had never invited me for dinner. Nevertheless, I would never have looked at her and figured her for a person I should borrow a gun from.

So, part of me wondering if I'd been set up, I got in touch with her one afternoon and inquired if she might, indeed, own a handgun.

"What are you looking for?" she asked.

"Um, I don't know," I said. "Just a handgun."

To narrow my choices, Susan calmly rattled off a list of weaponry she had on hand, from snub-nosed revolvers to rifles. I remember being bowled over when the word "Glock" came out of her very sophisticated mouth. The next day, she provided me with the gun she deemed best for my purposes.

You learn so little about people just from looking at them.

It's amazing, in a very unsatisfying way, how many snap judgments I can make about other people in just the course of a day—and how those judgments say more about me than they do about the folks I'm jumping to conclusions about.

It's an excellent lesson to remind myself of during a pandemic.

Later, I also learned that Susan had lived through horrific tragedy earlier in her life, something else I'd never have guessed based on our earlier interactions.

I was given a more serious reminder of how little appearances tell you not long after Susan helped me. I was staying in a hospital guest house in another city while my wife had surgery. The guest house had a common kitchen area; many of the folks staying there bought groceries and fixed meals there.

During my week-long stay, we did our best not to get in each other's way in the kitchen and sometimes ended up sitting and eating together.

One very pleasant and cheerful woman told me about her husband's double-lung transplant, from which he was still recovering and without which he would have quickly died. Another couple told me their forty-something son had just had part of a cancerous lung removed. Grimly, the father also told me that his son, who had smoked for thirty years, was unable to stop.

If I'd just encountered these folks in the elevator at the hospital, I would have had no idea of the level of suffering they were walking around with. And I might well have made some quick assessment of them, which would have certainly been unfairly and wholly inaccurate. We can't come close to knowing what's going on in someone's world when we're just outside looking in. The lives of strangers are a mystery, their pain often known to but a select few or borne alone.

So, back to COVID. The mask-wearing strangers we see now, from a distance, are even more difficult to read and understand than the strangers we encounter in "normal" times. And even when they're unmasked, I have no idea what toll this pandemic has taken on them, what losses they endured, what fears they carry with them.

So, let's be kind to one another. Let's try not to assume anything. For me, this requires serious heart surgery over and over. See you in the hospitality house.

Let's Talk—Or Maybe Not

I was a seventh grader when my parents decided it was time we had "the Talk." It was the 1970s, when it was easier to wait a little longer before holding that conversation. Still, Dad and Mom, like many parents of their generation, would probably rather have been poked in the eye with a stick than sit down and chat about the birds and the bees.

Nonetheless, Dad mustered his courage for this milestone in our parent-child relationship, sat me down in the room my brother and I shared, and began, "You've probably heard about this sex thing, haven't you?"

Not entirely sure if I was supposed to admit to that or not, I managed a quick nod. Dad then handed me a little paperback book called, I think, *A Baby is Born*, and after telling me he'd be back to see if I had any questions after I'd read it, he fled the scene.

When he returned a bit later and asked me if I wanted to talk about it, I vigorously shook my head no. And we were done, much to the relief of both of us.

It was a different era.

In recent conversations, I've learned Dad and Mom had been cheerfully sent down the aisle almost sixty years ago without a word on the subject of sex from either set of parents, as were some friends around my own age.

Those conversations got me to reminiscing about when—a while back now—the time came for me to play the role of the wise and all-knowing one in the Talk. Our son, Andy, was only in fourth grade, but a semi-ominous memo had come home with him from school, alerting us to some Family Life

144

Education activities headed his mostly-oblivious way.

"He's too young," I said to my wife.

"He's been asking questions," she responded. "Now you have a deadline." Thus ended the discussion.

We bought a book I hoped was much more user-friendly for both him and me than *A Baby is Born* had turned out to be. I liked it because it went beyond biological explanations and ventured into the moral perspective on sexual activity we wanted to include in our version of the Talk.

I set about preparing both Andy and myself, casually mentioning one day that I knew he had some questions about where babies came from and that I'd gotten a special book for us to read together soon. He responded with fairly resounding disinterest.

On the evening I'd appointed, he and I retreated to the bedroom and broke out the book. He was cool as a cucumber; I, on the other hand, have vague memories of consuming most of a bottle of Mylanta. We had really just gotten rolling when our oldest daughter, two years younger than Andy, used her ever-present antennae to discern something was up, opened the carefully shut door, and strolled in.

"Don't you knock before you come into a room when the door's closed?" I asked, somewhat pleasantly.

"You're just reading," she responded, and then launched into a brief interrogation about exactly what book it was that we were studying. I told her.

"Oh, that's just about babies in mommies' tummies and stuff," she said, not at all pleased, and promptly marched out, re-shutting the door.

Struggling to regain our momentum, I returned to the subject at hand, and Andy and I waded through the rest of the book together. His level of interest perked up some as we went, but never reached what anyone might describe as "fascinated."

As installment one of the Talk wound down, he pronounced,

"Sounds kinda icky, Dad." He's twenty-six now, and I'm fairly certain his feelings on the subject have changed somewhat.

He's our only son, so my wife got to take the lead in chatting with our daughters. That turned out to be a somewhat hilarious joint session that happened not too long after my evening with Andy, as the girls were determined not to remain uninformed about a subject their brother already knew a little about.

Looking back, those are precious memories for my wife and me. In today's world, we parental types really do need to step up for the Talk, as awkward as it can feel. The stakes are so, so high, and there are so many other ways, mostly very unhelpful ones, in which kids today can get this information.

Not long after Andy and I's Talk, my wife asked him about it. "We had fun," he told her. In retrospect, I have to agree—and I'm glad the evening was Mylanta-free for one of us.

What Will We Learn from COVID?

Sometimes life just rolls through, like an unstoppable force, and leaves us off-balance, jarred out of our routines, and more than a bit jumpy. In my experience, that has almost always meant that I'm being presented with the opportunity to learn something. Seems like we glean most of our really meaningful insights when life is hard. Don't know why that has to be, but it is.

So, what are we going to learn from the coronavirus?

Life is so very changed, and it seems to have become that way so very quickly. I write this a couple days after what was a very subdued St. Patrick's Day here in Richmond, as we washed our hands and kept our social distance. If hindsight helps us see and understand more clearly, how will we think of this time when next St. Patrick's Day comes around? How will we be different?

Endurance can be a great teacher because it can take us farther than we normally push ourselves. Most of us, though, aren't out running marathons. (That's because when confronted with a trip of 26.2 miles, we do the reasonable thing—drive.) We will, though, endure COVID-19 together. Yes, together, though many of us are largely home-bound.

And together, we've lost so much already. We no longer live with the sense of freedom and security we once did. We're wary of things we didn't give a second thought to a couple months ago. We've lost much of the spontaneity that can make life so interesting and fun. And we've got cabin fever. Bad.

We've also lost some of what makes Richmond so great. There weren't thousands of us on Monument Avenue running in and supporting the 10K in March. There may be in September. Our museums are closed; we missed out on Michelle Obama and Bryan Stevenson, two great guests slated for the Richmond Forum; our farmer's markets have been canceled. We've lost a film festival, art events, benefit events for local nonprofits, and theater performances. We can't meet up with friends and family and eat at our great restaurants. We can't go to church or, largely, to work. Inexplicably, we can't seem to get enough toilet paper to meet our suddenly insatiable needs.

And let's not even talk about March Madness.

However, to be frank, most of that falls under the category of inconvenience. We can learn to do without a lot of things. But some of us are feeling the sting of COVID-19 in ways that are far more than inconvenient. Restaurant workers and other employees in small businesses have lost their jobs. As I write, a growing number of us are testing positive for the virus. Lives are being disrupted in very frightening ways.

Some of what we are suffering is very real; some may just feel real. I've read that suffering is wasted if we grit our teeth and just fight it until it's over, and I think it's true. Suffering is useful when we come out of it different than when we went in. What can we take away from all this? I can't answer that, and many of us may never know. But there is something we might consider taking now, as we experience it.

Notes.

Was Elvis an Angel?

"People don't take trips—trips take people," wrote novelist John Steinbeck, a guy who would know: He traveled extensively and also served as a World War II correspondent throughout Europe.

I, on the other hand, have done very little international travel.

Thus, as my plane recently landed in an absolutely spectacular Central American country, I congratulated myself on how smoothly the first two legs of the journey had gone, particularly in light of Hurricane Julia, who was cruising along nearby. All that remained was a multiple-hour layover and a short puddle-jumper flight on a local airline before I met our first grandchild.

I chatted with a fellow passenger, a native who spoke English, as we checked in. Sadly, my Spanish goes no further than Mexican restaurant menus. During the long afternoon, therefore, after each of the many terminal flight announcements, I'd make eye contact with him and he'd shake his head, saying, "Not us."

The airline itself steadfastly maintained radio silence about the status of our flight as the hours went by and the weather began to look more threatening, and from where we were situated, we couldn't see if there was an actual plane at our gate or not.

Just a couple minutes before our scheduled departure, the woman who had checked us in briefly appeared at the gate, sending a surge of hope through the fifteen or so of us passengers-to-be. She was chatting on her cell phone, though, a conversation that continued as she casually left the gate without a word to us.

After another hour-plus rolled by, another announcement alerted my check-in buddy, and thus me, that not only was our flight canceled but that the airport was closing because Julia's rain was arriving. Our alleged airline kicked into full-on customer service mode, basically telling us, "Take your luggage and leave the airport immediately." Darkness was now falling, as was rain, and the city we were in—thanks to traditional local festivities including drug trafficking and gang activity—had once been rated the second most dangerous on the planet.

Let's just say I was not eager to wander around in said city looking like a confused tourist.

Check-in pal, who I now knew was named Elvis, announced he wasn't spending another night anywhere before he got home. He'd been gone for five months, part of an oil rig crew in Africa, and was rather eager to see his wife and three kids again. As we strategized, an American couple joined the chat. They were with a missionary organization, traveled around supporting their people on the ground, and this was not their first encounter with travel gone awry. The four of us decided our best bet was to rent a car and make the three-hour drive to where our flight had been bound, hometown to Elvis. We anointed him both navigator and translator, as the couple's Spanish skills rivaled my own.

God tends to show up in other folks, some we know and some we don't.

The airport's first rental desk was rapidly closing and shooed us away. The next one was happy to help if we were happy to provide them with a deposit of $1,600. We weren't, but we did anyway.

So, the four of us set out in a loaded-down Kia, me at the wheel, and we immediately took the wrong exit ramp, which somewhat damaged our faith in Elvis. One semi-quick and probably semi-legal U-turn remedied the situation—at least

in terms of being headed in the proper direction.

We rode two-lane roads the rest of the way and, as it was a holiday weekend, we were joined there by countless pedestrians (including many children), cyclists of both the motor and pedal variety, lots of dogs (so many dogs, so few leash laws), and an occasional horse, none of whom seemed to believe in, much less sport, reflective devices or clothing.

No speed limit was posted, but our pace was soon monitored by what Elvis called the "sleeping police." This is a truly diabolical system of sometimes lethal speed bumps that appear without warning when it's dark. What followed can only be described as bone-jarring, prompting my hapless passengers to mention how happy they were that *they* hadn't plunked down the deposit. One announced that she was going to "focus on my reading" and briefly went nose-in-book, an enormously ineffective plan.

Truth be told, it was a surprisingly fun outing, with great company and no carnage. Eventually, we dropped the couple at their hotel and got Elvis reunited with his family (including five-year-old Elvis Jr.). I successfully found my wife and son-in-law at, logically, a Pizza Hut, and the rest of the week went brilliantly.

Days later, we returned after midnight to the parking deck at the Richmond airport to discover our car's battery had died. Yeah. This trip definitely took me.

Merry Christmas!

We don't sing about it in any of the carols, and it's not mentioned in any of the biblical accounts of the birth of Jesus, but this little story about a seven-year-old boy in South Carolina does about as good a job of summing up Christmas as any story I know.

Writer Brennan Manning says the boy's mother was so occupied wrapping Christmas presents that she asked him to shine her shoes so they'd be ready for church the next day. He worked diligently and then proudly brought the shiny results of his labor to her. She was so pleased with the job he'd done she gave him a quarter.

But when she slipped on the shoes the next morning, she felt an uncomfortable lump in one of them and pulled it back off. Inside, she discovered the quarter, wrapped in a scribbled-on piece of paper.

"I done it for love," read the note.

Sounds like Christmas in five words, to me. On this day every December, we celebrate the birth of an obscure infant in an obscure country, which took place in a grubby stable that stunk of farm animals and lacked heat and air, not to mention decent health care. Why the celebration?

He done it for love.

Jesus, who created the cosmos and had it and so much more to hang around in, came to Earth and confined himself to human form for a few decades. He gave up a life unimaginable to us to live as a man—a baby, even. He done it for love.

While he was here, he lunched with society's outcasts, actually touched lepers, healed the sick, taught the people, defied corrupt authorities, walked on water, showed us how to live, and offered a way to a life beyond this one. He done it for love.

Oh yeah, while he was here he also suffered an excruciating and voluntary death, and spent three days in a tomb. He done it for love, and he wouldn't have accepted our quarter.

"If there is any meaning in the life of Jesus of Nazareth, it is this: that there is a God who created us, and who loves us so much he would stop at nothing to bring us to him," wrote the late singer Rich Mullins. "If Jesus means anything, he means you are loved."

It all began in a stable, the one we remember today. He done it for love. Merry Christmas.

Happy Easter!

Just about everyone is familiar with the cross; it may be the most recognizable symbol on the planet. Crosses appear on everything from buildings to books to bumper stickers, and many Christians wear one on a chain around their necks. As I type, I'm wearing a ring with a cross on it. Crosses are so common that for many, they've become a cool fashion accessory or a nice thought.

I want very much to avoid thinking of a cross that way because, in truth, there's nothing cool, fashionable, or nice about it.

Crosses became famous as instruments of pain and death. During a time in history when "cruel and unusual" actually seemed to be the goal of most executions, crucifixion was considered so barbaric that the Roman Emperor Constantine abolished it in the fourth century.

The cross is a very hard thing. I admit that while I've been a follower of Jesus for years now, I still struggle to get my mind and heart around the events of this, the week leading up to Easter Sunday. Did Jesus really have to do this? Wasn't there any other way he could have demonstrated the depth of his love for us, and the brokenness of the way we so often live our lives?

I have heard, over the years, plenty of attempts to intellectually explain why the death of Jesus had to happen, and have even made some of those attempts myself. But I've never really been able to love those explanations, or even like most of them very much. Jesus' death was so painful and gory, his rejection and humiliation so complete. How do I rejoice in that?

Yet, next Sunday I will join millions of other believers around the world to celebrate Easter, the most joyful day of the Christian year. And I'll do so with happy conviction, a clear conscience, and, I hope, real joy.

Two things, over time, have helped me get past my questions about and resistance to the crucifixion and reach a place where Easter can truly be a joyous occasion.

One is that Jesus was the most others-centered human ever—everything he did was about healing, teaching, and guiding us, and ultimately setting us free. He came here purely for us, proclaiming he "came not to be served, but to serve and give [my] life as a ransom for many."

Every major religion has a fundamental understanding that our deepest, truest joy comes when our focus shifts from putting ourselves first to putting others first.

"Our happiness comes to us only when we do not seek for it," is how philosophy professor and Christian writer Peter Kreeft puts this. "It comes to us when we seek others' happiness instead."

So Jesus had us in mind in everything he did. The second thing that's been very helpful to me is something I heard a pastor for whom I have the greatest respect say a few years back. I don't have the exact words in my head, but the gist of it was "maybe we should think of it less as Jesus *had* to die for us than that Jesus *chose* to die for us."

Every major religion also acknowledges that the greatest joys of our lives often grow out of suffering. The metaphor frequently used is that the pain of childbirth is followed by the joy of new life, but the principle extends beyond the delivery room.

What if, in dying, and in making redemption, new life, and real joy possible for us, Jesus not only accomplished the greatest rescue ever, but also experienced ultimate joy, the kind that comes from what he described as the greatest form of love—laying down your life for another?

Maybe these words from famed Christian writer and Nazi resister Dietrich Bonhoeffer are true of both us and Jesus himself: "To go one's way under the sign of the cross is not misery and desperation, but peace and refreshment for the soul; it is the highest joy."

I hope my ring at least occasionally reminds me of that.

Happy Mother's Day!

Mothers are fonder than fathers of their children because they are more certain they are their own. — Aristotle

My mom began having children back when women were rendered unconscious for the occasion and fathers paced somewhere far from where the action was taking place. When her first was born, Mom woke up in a recovery room and had to flag down a passing orderly to find out what she'd had. He disappeared for a moment and then returned to tell her that she now had a son. Apparently, she took this as good news because she had two more children in the next two years. Three children under three caused her ability to put together a coherent sentence to briefly desert her and so the next three kids were a bit more spaced out—literally, and I might add, since I know them well, figuratively as well.

Mom was conscious when her final child was born, but Dad was at home tending to the rest of us. I stood next to him as he fielded the phone call from the hospital informing him that he'd had his fourth daughter, a piece of news that left me crestfallen.

If evolution really works, how come mothers only have two hands? — Milton Berle

Any mother could perform the jobs of several air traffic controllers with ease. — Lisa Alther

Once she had kids, Mom stepped out of her nurse's uniform and didn't work outside the home again for a good thirty years—but no one ever worked harder inside it. If she'd been paid what she was worth in the corporate world, she'd have been knocking down six figures back in the 1960s, when that was serious money. A typical day for her in my youth began with an assembly line of sandwiches for school lunches (during which she patiently endured massive whining, requests, and complaints) and proceeded through several hundred loads of laundry, hours of housework, a little unenthusiastic pet care, grocery shopping, cooking, carpooling, homework-overseeing, disciplining, making sure her offspring were properly clothed, and managing several bedtime rituals. And she did all this while maintaining a Nobel-like level of diplomacy skills in a household often at a young-person high-decibel and high-conflict level. It's an accomplishment, in my mind, that in her seventies she still has enough working brain cells to faithfully tackle the daily Jumble.

Sweater, n.: garment worn by a child when its mother is feeling chilly. — Ambrose Bierce

This one actually worked in reverse in my house. Mom hates liver, and as a result never forced it on her children. To this day, I have never had a bite of liver—or kidney, pancreas, spleen, or any other organ that I'm sure God never intended to be consumed. She did, however, force fish sticks upon us on many Fridays, for which I have just recently forgiven her. As a result, today fish sticks are to my children as liver is to me.

A suburban mother's role is to deliver children obstetrically once, and by car forever after. — Peter De Vries

Mom wore out a series of station wagons dragging us up and down the road, and never seemed to lose her way. However, I'm told that it was while filling up at a gas station that she came closest to murder, when an attendant, seeing three of us asleep in the back of the wagon, remarked, "Nice litter."

She got to where she was going quickly, but I think she's yet to get her first speeding ticket. Not long ago, though, she was nearly permanently blinded one night by the flash of the camera that photographed her license plate as she inadvertently drove through a red light.

Is my mother my friend? I would have to say, first of all she is my Mother, with a capital 'M'; she's something sacred to me. I love her dearly...yes, she is also a good friend, someone I can talk openly with if I want to. – Sophia Loren

Mom will always be older and wiser, but nowadays she's also become a really wonderful friend—picking up the phone and hearing her voice is one of my life's great pleasures. Not only do we have my entire life in common, now we have parenting in common, too. I enjoy her amusement at my attempts to keep my children on the straight and narrow, and my kids love to see her when she comes to town.

She's always had a comforting, supportive way about her, and even now, talking with Mom still makes things seem just a bit better. I want her around for as long as I can have her.

My mom is a neverending song in my heart of comfort, happiness and being. I may sometimes forget the words but I always remember the tune. – Graycie Harmon

Enough said.

Happy Father's Day!

Father's Day has turned up again, and the merchants of America have been busily suggesting ways we offspring might demonstrate our love and esteem for Dad. Maybe it's just my perverse nature, but it somehow makes sense to look at the gift-giving the other way around.

The gifts my father has given me are a whole lot more meaningful—and longer lasting—than any of the books and shirts he's gotten from me on Sundays in June. In thousands of small moments, he's given me enough to last a lifetime.

He gave me perspective in one fleeting instant. A cocky teenager with a learner's permit, I was whizzing through a darkening, late afternoon rainstorm in New Jersey, Dad patiently riding shotgun.

"You got your lights on?" he asked.

"I can see fine," I replied, way too smugly.

"Can anybody see you?"

With a quick question, he helped me understand that maybe my life isn't entirely about me.

He taught me what it means to put my family first. After Dad got a job transfer when we were all elementary schoolers or younger, he looked hard for a community that had what he wanted for his wife and children. Finding one, he made it our home—and while we got great memories, he got a frustrating, grueling commute for the next sixteen years.

One summer while we were living there, he and Mom packed a pop-up trailer and five kids and took us on a three-week extravaganza out west, to places including Yellowstone and the Grand Canyon. None of us will ever forget those places, or the gumption it took to undertake such a trip.

He showed me what it means to be committed to a marriage. There have been the inevitable tough times in Dad and Mom's more than half-century together, but we all knew there was never any real danger that they wouldn't be together until the end. Having a front-row seat for that kind of commitment later helped dispel a lot of my own prenuptial jitters.

He opened new possibilities by convincing me not to sell myself short. Too young to get a "real" summer job, I was offered a junior camp counselor position for very meager pay following my first year in high school. I was prepared to take it when Dad encouraged me to run an ad in the local paper offering my handyman and lawn care services. I ran the ad— and made ten times what the camp would have paid me.

He showed me faith, in his own unassuming way. I don't remember sermons, but I do remember not digging into meals without praying first. And somehow, no matter what obscure spot we'd find ourselves in on a weekend, we always found a church. I was once scolded by a woman in Maine for being barefoot in a small country church, having just climbed out of a boat. (She told me she wouldn't go to a laundromat that way, let alone the house of the Lord.) What that lady didn't know, and what I was too intimidated to tell her, is that Dad brought us in early so we could be there.

You can't capture a man in a few isolated incidents. But, taken together, they can point you in the right direction. Through all the stages of my life, I think that's what Dad has been trying most to do—point me in the right direction. Despite my frequent attempts to foil him, I think he's done a pretty impressive job. And I've come to love and respect him more than any man I've ever met.

What it all comes down to is that I can't really give Dad a thing. For the rest of my life, I'll be unwrapping and using the things he's given me.

Maybe, if this Father's Day he sees just a few glimpses of that, it will be enough.

About Atmosphere Press

Founded in 2015, Atmosphere Press was built on the principles of Honesty, Transparency, Professionalism, Kindness, and Making Your Book Awesome. As an ethical and author-friendly hybrid press, we stay true to that founding mission today.

If you're a reader, enter our giveaway for a free book here:

SCAN TO ENTER
BOOK GIVEAWAY

If you're a writer, submit your manuscript for consideration here:

SCAN TO SUBMIT
MANUSCRIPT

And always feel free to visit Atmosphere Press and our authors online at atmospherepress.com. See you there soon!

About the Author

TOM ALLEN has written about health, education, sports, and other topics for 35 years and was a regular contributor to the Faith & Values column of the *Richmond Times-Dispatch* for more than a decade. His writing has appeared in newspapers and magazines across Virginia and in other publications, including the *Pittsburgh Post-Gazette*. Since 1990, he has served as the editor of the *Virginia Journal of Education*.

Allen's first book, *Grace Happens: Adventures in Everyday Living*, was published in 2017.

He lives in Richmond with his wife, Cathy. They have three grown children and have now acquired two in-law children and a granddaughter.

You can contact Tom at tomed1@hotmail.com.

Printed in Great Britain
by Amazon

32385294R00101